SARAH,

Semper
Fidelis

Life after Death

A Survivor's Story

Brad C. Fite

To Brixton Matthew Fite

You are the brightest light after the deepest darkness.
You are my life after death.
You are my legacy.
You are my son.
I love you.

CONTENTS

ACKNOWLEDGMENTS

First and foremost I would like to thank you, Aimee, for loving me relentlessly and fighting for me when I couldn't. Thank you for being the most wonderful part of the rest of my tomorrows.

Thank you, Mom, Dad, Bryce, BJ, Sarah, Lindsay, and David for loving me unconditionally.

Thank you, Paul DeGelder, for your friendship and for inspiring me to dream beyond what I ever thought possible. I would not have made it through the darkness without the light you provided for me.

Thank you, AJ Anderson, for your love, support, and friendship. No matter where I was, you had my six. No matter how low I fell, you reached to pick me up.

Thank you, Barry Boswell, for being my best friend and never letting me go through anything alone.

Thank you to my Mighty Oaks Warrior Program brothers for having the strength and willingness to conquer your fears and heal your wounds with me. Thank you for all the love and support that you have shown me. Thank you for always having my six. Burn the ships.

INTRODUCTION

On this day, to you, I indulge in honesty. For the greater part of the last four years of my life, I have been talking to and living with the dead; it is time for me to reach out and be among the living. I have been in hiding and isolation to escape the mindless judgment that I feared was at every corner in my ever-twisting story. The ink I am bleeding out onto this paper is truth—and this I swear: it is nothing but. For the first time in years, I feel like I can be open and honest. In these words I fear no judgment and feel no remorse. I simply bleed this ink until my pen is dry.

I am terrified as I write this to you. I am afraid that my writing is not good enough. I am afraid of being seen as weak. I am afraid to share my story; in my story are my deepest and darkest secrets. In telling this story I am forced to relive some of the most horrifying days of my life, and I'm afraid that I am not ready for that. In all honestly, I will never be ready.

But ready or not, it's time. It's time for you to know Bradley Christian Fite: the man, the Marine, the wounded, the killer, the addict, the monster, and greatest of all, the survivor.

In suffocating my thoughts and drowning my emotions, I became a monster—one that I hated but could not seem to escape. The day I realized that I hated myself was a day of dark awakening. I couldn't look at myself in the mirror. It was a place of such deep torment that I would wish it on no one.

Hate is a monstrous emotion, capable of driving the most sickening actions. The torturous prison of hatred seems impossible to walk away from. To escape, you will find yourself, at best, crawling on your hands and knees, and when you are far enough away, the overwhelming power of love will help you stand.

> *Today I am still crawling. But crawling is movement; movement is key to survival, and in survival, there is hope.*

At the darkest moment of my life, I discovered that I was embedded in hate. Today I am still crawling. But crawling is movement; movement is key to survival, and in survival, there is hope. The existence of this hope is why I am streaming my tears into words.

As a combat Marine, I was taught the art of survival. I was taught to survive, but I was not taught to hope. And I have done a great deal of hopeless survival in my days. Hope is succulent, delicious, and alive. It navigates its way through your veins and ignites the soul. Hope is at the crux of survival.

As you pilot your way through my words, I pray that they give you hope and awaken in you the fiercest appetite for life. These pages are joyfully and fearfully written with the ink of a bleeding heart, but a bleeding heart is a beating heart.

This is *my* bleeding heart.

BRAD C. FITE

LIFE AFTER DEATH

Before I was a tactically trained combat-operational Marine—and way before my world became 360 degrees of pure, uncontrolled chaos—I was an untamed kid with a zest for adventure, usually at the cost of a few broken bones. A skinned knee and sidewalk burns just weren't enough for me. I lived on the wild side, always pushing the limit.

Most six-year-old boys see their first bicycle as a cool new toy. I saw mine as a first-class ticket to the Wild, Wild West. It wasn't just another Huffy; it was a limitless two-wheeled stallion—a man-making machine. I remember sitting in the garage, peering from a distance, trying my hardest to contain my eager anticipation as I watched my dad unwind the screws that were holding the training wheels.

I looked out into the street and carefully planned and visualized my first route: I would take off, seamlessly, like I was a born rider on a direct course to freedom—the humid summer breeze at my back and the hot Michigan sun on my determined face. I had watched my older brother ride his two-wheeler, and he would always jump over a certain pothole that plagued the parking lot of the park across the street from our house. I didn't want to settle for an ordinary first ride. I wanted to jump that pothole and earn some street cred from my bro. My dad loaded me up and gave me a push. I took off like a fighter jet down the runway, and I *was* a natural!

I approached the enemy pothole with grit and purpose; it was now the only thing standing in the way of greatness. I pulled up on my handlebars like I had watched my brother do time and time again, but instead of my bike *and* me flying majestically through the sky over the pothole, my front tire went straight down, lodged deep in the depths of rock and debris, and I flew over the pothole alone. My bike crashed into the ground, and I skidded face first into the hot, sun-scorched black pavement. It was a two-wheeled massacre. Thus began a regular trend of injury.

For some reason, I continually landed myself—and one or both of my parents—in the emergency room, awaiting my next X-ray. I didn't count down days to birthdays; I counted down days until whatever cast I was in came off or whatever injury I sustained was healed.

I was drawn to the rush of competition, whether it was a simple—yet somehow always dangerous— game of Ping-Pong with my brother or any one of my three varsity sports in high school. The invigorating feeling of victory and the stinging pain of loss kept me searching for more. After two broken feet my senior year and my fourth (maybe fifth or sixth—it's debatable) solid concussion that came from an eighty-eight-mile-per-hour fastball to my head, I began fighting.

Mixed martial arts (MMA) was becoming a little more known in certain areas, and as it grew into sport, I wanted in. I started training in a small Brazilian jujitsu gym in Allen Park, Michigan, and followed the sport far into my college days. I trained every day, and I excelled quickly. My first three fights were little rinky-dink, hole-in-the-wall-type bouts, but the thrill of stepping into the cage and hearing the applause of the crowd was a high that I never even knew existed.

I didn't fight because I was angry or because I craved violence; I fought because I loved the rush of the sport. Little did I know then, as a young eighteen-year-old kid, but in the future, fighting would not only be the near death of me; it would also be my only ticket to survival.

With my new love for fighting and after watching the tragic, historic collapse of the Twin Towers on September 11, 2001, my desire to join the military was ignited. I had always had a love for flying, and what cooler job in the world could there be than to be a fighter pilot? I joined the Air Force and went to college to pursue my commission through the University of Michigan's ROTC program.

After only a year of school, my wandering spirit (mixed with a little bit of trouble) led me to Liberty University, in Lynchburg, Virginia. The plan remained the same: achieve a pilot's slot and obtain my commission. But hey, a college kid's gotta have fun too!

I was a really smart kid—though at the time my grades didn't necessarily show it—and after completing my first semester at Liberty, I was offered a unique opportunity to take part in a prestigious internship in Washington, DC. I jumped at the chance to move to DC, and at the opening of 2008, I packed my bags and moved from Virginia to the nation's capital. I worked for Congressman Joe Wilson (R) of South Carolina's 2nd District. The job was the most fun I'd ever had, and I even had an accidental collision with (then) Senator Barrack Obama in the tunnels below the Senate.

I was working all day, trying to study all evening, and still partying all night with my best friend and roommate, Barry. It was working out almost too well. I was great at my job and excelled in my ROTC program, every day getting closer and closer to my pilot's slot. Late one evening, I logged in to my student account for my Liberty online classes and saw that I had an e-mail from an old fight friend of mine. He was writing to let me know that our team had a big fight night coming up, and their lightweight fighter had dropped out. He asked me if there was any way that I would be able to make it back to Detroit in only a few weeks to fight at 130 pounds. My heart managed to sink and jump at the same time. I wanted that fight—I *really* wanted that fight—but there was just no way I could make it happen.

Or was there?

Despite the numerous red flags, I flew home to Michigan and had less than a week to train, lose over twenty pounds, and prepare for my bout. I spent every single day tirelessly wrecking my body to cut weight but still trying my hardest to prepare myself for combat. I was exhausting every ounce of power I had and was worried that come fight night, I might make weight, but I wouldn't have enough energy left to fight.

Fight night came, and though I was feeling weak and unprepared, I headed to the venue in Detroit. I was the fourth fight on the ticket, and when my time came, Rage Against the Machine's "Pistol Grip Pump" came blaring out over the speakers. As the crowd erupted, I felt it again: I felt the rush of pure adrenaline coursing through my veins.

My tired eyes darkened with a fierce passion for victory as I approached the cage. The only thing on my mind now was winning.

I woke up a few hours later in the hospital, my face wrapped in gauze and my concerned parents sitting beside my bed. I asked them what was going on and kept insisting that they let me go, because I had to get to my fight. I remembered nothing of the entire evening's events, but I'm sure you've guessed by now that I did not win the fight.

I went into surgery, and the left side of my face was reconstructed and reinforced with titanium plates. It was only the first of many surgeries that I would face in the near future. Due to my facial reconstruction and the substantial damage to the orbital bone just below my eye, I was disqualified from attending flight school, and I lost my scholarship. This ultimately resulted in the ending of my blossoming and hopeful career in the Air Force.

I dropped out of college after falling significantly behind in my studies, and I moved back to Michigan. I didn't have time to be depressed about my situation; I just needed to figure out what was next.

When I had first approached my dad about joining the military, I had told him that I wanted to enlist in the Marine Corps. His eyes had widened, and after taking no time at all to think about his next words, he had told me no, that I should join the Air Force. I had fought him a little, but in the end, we had agreed that getting a college degree would be nice. So I went with the Air Force. Now, with that option long gone, all I could think about was joining the Marines.

I knew that going back to school wasn't for me, and I definitely wasn't going to join the Army, because even before I was a Marine I was a cocky son of a gun, and in my head I was already picturing myself in those storied dress blues. I drove over to the recruiter's station and walked directly into the Marines office.

My stroll toward the Marines office inside the recruiting station didn't come without a valiant effort from both the Army and the Navy trying to snag me first. The Army grabbed me, offered to pay for all my school debt, and even offered me a nice signing bonus. Directly across the hall was the Navy, and they said that I could be a SEAL. The Marines offered me one thing: "We'll make you a Marine."

The recruiter sat in front of me, dressed to kill in his service uniform, and began asking me questions about my past and what I wanted in my future. He asked me about my drug history: none. He asked me about my criminal record: none. He asked me about school, and I gave him my transcripts. He then asked about my health problems, to which I replied, "None...well...except a reconstructed face. I shattered the left side of my face in a cage fight about five months ago."

He asked me if I could see, and I said yes.

Then he said, "Okay, let's get this thing going. When are you looking to get outta here?"

"As soon as possible."

A little less than three weeks later I was shipped off to Parris Island Recruit Depot, where I would be molded into one of America's finest fighting machines—a Marine. As my recruiter dropped me off at the hotel where I would stay the night before my flight to South Carolina, he shook my hand and said, "Go be extraordinary."

"Yes, sir."

***

From the first second of the very first day, I was hooked. I loved it: the screaming, the yelling, the running, the sweating, the chaos, the pride, the push-ups, the sandpits, the push-ups in the sandpits, the screaming and yelling while you're doing push-ups in the sandpits, the god-awful food, the screaming, the yelling, the shooting, the marching, the screaming, the insanity of the drill instructors, the molding, and ultimately everything that went into the making of a Marine. I loved every bit of it.

Upon graduation, I was given my military occupational specialty (MOS) of 1833, amphibious assault (YAT-YAS!). The next few months were spent learning and mastering my trade.

After all my basic schooling was complete, I was given orders to 3rd Amphibious Assault Battalion, aboard Camp Pendleton, CA. I excelled quickly, and it wasn't long until my first promotion. I had made a name for myself in my platoon as a fighter, and I took every opportunity I had to master the different levels of belts of the Marine Corps martial arts system. I also made it very clear that the only reason I was in the Marines was to go to war. I was a fighter, and I was here to fight. I spent every spare moment I had in the gym, working out and preparing my body for the ultimate test.

My platoon sergeant, Staff Sergeant Corbett, approached me one morning and pulled me aside after our formation.

> *He just shook his head, saddened, and looked at me like I was already dead.*

"Fite, before you answer this question, I want you to think very carefully. Do you still want to go to war?"

I didn't have to think. A genuine and indisputable yes shot from my mouth almost before he could even end his question. He nodded his head and handed me my military record file.

"Go check out of Charlie Company." He paused and gritted his teeth down, almost as if trying to hold the words back from coming out. But with another nod he continued and said, "Check into Bravo. You're goin' to Afghanistan." He shook my hand, and I was off.

Before I checked out of Charlie Company, I ran over to my crew chief's amtrac and hopped in the back.

I sat there next to Corporal AJ Anderson and asked him one simple thing: "Corporal Anderson, what's war like?"

He had been deployed to Iraq a few years previous, and he and I had formed a good relationship since I had checked in, so I figured that he would be the guy to ask.

He just shook his head, saddened, and looked at me like I was already dead.

It is with great honor that I compile these next few pages of mere words. I am going to tell you about some of the greatest men that I have ever known—men who day in and day out laid it all on the line for their brothers. I am so proud to call these men my brothers, and it is with the deepest gratitude that I can sit here now and write about them.

**To my team, for saving my life, and
to Corporal Julio Vargas,
for sacrificing yours**

*"Greater love hath no man than this,
that a man lay down his life for his friends."*
—John 15:13

I write this for:

**Lieutenant Colonel Jay Erwin
Sergeant Chris Falzone
Sergeant Terrence Williams
Corporal Alejandro Sanchez
Corporal Matthew Miles
Corporal John Galvan
Corporal Reed Frodin
Corporal Patrick Tunney
Corporal Oscar Montanez
Corporal Jake Asp
Corporal Will Pruett
Corporal Aaron Arceneaux
Corporal Jose Lobos
Doc Nick Mervau**

We deployed in the burning summer heat at the peak of the war on terror, into the heart of Taliban-occupied Marjah, Afghanistan, in the southern province of Helmand.

July 19, 2010, was a typical day. Our team took a routine patrol through Marjah's bazaar and checked in on the Afghanistan army's checkpoints to make sure that everything was operating smoothly. My spot in the patrol was in the fourth team, and I was the machine gun operator. My trusted SAW 249 and I were the muscle in the back of the formation.

Each day, as soon as the sun would set and the fiery heat of the day would die down, I would make my way to the improvised desert gym. It started out with sandbags and an uneven pull-up bar, but eventually it became a remarkably efficient workout zone. Working out and lifting weights was my time to relieve stress, and it was a little taste of home for me.

That night I did my makeshift, CrossFit-inspired workout and lifted weights with a lieutenant colonel who was stationed with us. Then I headed over to the well with my bucket and soap for a quick shower. My mom made sure to send me plenty of care packages, complete with ample amounts of body soap. (Mothers need to know that their sons are keeping good hygiene while in dirty, rugged combat!) And I am a huge supporter of a long, hot shower. Over there, it was a maximum of ten minutes—if you knew how to regulate your bucket pours.

After my shower that night, I went to my tent to grab a guitar that a chaplain had donated to my camp, and then I sat on the hood of one of the trucks to write in my journal and play some music.

The days over there were brutally hot. The sun would beat down on us relentlessly, but at night, the scene was surprisingly spectacular. It was breathtaking, I swear: you could see every single star shining in that Afghanistan sky. There were no streetlights, and there was no glare from cities to deter the dark. There didn't seem to be a cloud in the sky. It was just desert, mountains, and beautiful stars, shining for miles and miles, surrounding the biggest, clearest moon I've ever seen. I sat there and wondered how a place so evil and ugly could transform into such beauty in a matter of minutes. Just when I would begin to enjoy the natural splendor of the country, the echoing boom of a distant bomb exploding would rattle the earth, and it would snap me out of my hopeful delusions.

That night, I enjoyed a small amount of peace, looking into the sky full of stars as I wrote about the day's activities and accomplishments. I put my journal down and strummed out a few chords on the fourth-hand, gifted guitar.

A while later, I headed into my crowded tent and hopped onto my cot. Bedtime. For some reason, I couldn't seem to sleep, so I made my way back over to our gym and tried tiring myself out. The sweltering heat of the day had burned down to a balmy mid-90 degrees and felt almost cold in comparison to the Afghani summer sun. This change in temperature was refreshing and cultivated in me an incredible second wind—as opposed to the initial goal of tiring me out.

My platoon commander, Lt. Goetz, was also unable to sleep that night and meandered his way over to the gym. I was doing one of my original

"CrossFite" workouts, and Lt. Goetz joined in. We worked out, listened to music, and talked about our lives back home for hours. After we exhausted the last of our evening's second wind, we both hit the cots and tried for a couple hours of shut-eye.

July 20, 2010, commenced before dawn. We were awake, gearing up, and staging our trucks for the day's mission. Our squad leader, Sgt. Falzone, gathered the squad to brief us on our mission, just as he had for every other mission that we had completed.

Our mission on July 20, 2010, was to safely escort the hopeful and revolutionary governor of Marjah and certain key military leaders to a governmental meeting just seven miles north of base.

That morning we headed out in four fully combat-armored vehicles. Our squad was made up of four fire teams, each having its own vehicle and a heavy-machine-gun operator perched in the swiveling turret.

One of the vehicles was longer than the others, and it was the one assigned to transport the governor and his assistant leaders. Each vehicle was strategically placed in a particular order to maximize each fire team's full potential.

The first vehicle was Falzone's. He had a driver, a gunner, and a communications Marine, and he was in the passenger seat, navigating every route, sending up reports, and keeping communication with the other vehicles. That truck also had a mine roller, which was a lifesaving tool attached to the front of it, designed to put an ample amount of force to the earth's surface and made to detonate any improvised explosive devices (IEDs) that were triggered by pressure.

The second vehicle was made up of another fire team. The fire-team leader sat in the passenger seat. He had a gunner and a driver.

The third vehicle was the longest of the four. It held my workout buddy, Lt. Col. Jay Erwin. Cpl. Galvan, the assistant squad leader, was in the passenger seat, and the vehicle included a .40mm gunner, Cpl. Matt Miles, a driver, the Marjah governor and his assistants, and other key military personnel that attended the meeting with him on that day. Our corpsman, Doc Mervau, sat in the back.

The fourth vehicle was mine. I was the gunner, meaning that I stood in the turret and operated the .50 caliber machine gun that was mounted on the roof of the truck. Cpl. Sanchez was driving with Sgt. Williams, my fire-team leader, in the passenger seat up front. Cpl. Julio Vargas was in the back of the truck. Not only was Julio an incredible Marine, but he was also a highly skilled medic, so having him as our rear dismount Marine was very tactically effective.

It was only seven miles north up the road, and it took us about forty minutes to get there. When we pulled into the other base, we parked our massive trucks in a temporary staging area. The governor and his party exited the vehicles so that they could get to their meeting, which was supposed to last a couple hours.

About six hours later, the meeting let out, and everyone came back to the trucks, tired and ready to head back to home base. I was sitting in the back of the truck with Julio, trying my best to escape the 120-degree heat, and we were listening to Zac Brown Band's "Foundation" album while snacking on beef jerky and sunflower seeds. We got the word to start prepping for departure, so I strapped into my harness and took my place in the turret. Julio locked my harness into the floor while I prepped my .50 cal. The governor and his party were loaded in and ready to roll. Radio checks between the team's trucks were underway. I switched my iPod on to Rage Against the Machine and began my mental preparation. Right as we were about to head out, Julio tugged on my leg.

"Brad, hey Brad! Let me take the turret for the ride back—"

"Dude," I interrupted, "we're about to leave; it's fine."

"I know; just switch me. You've been up there all day."

"Julio, we are literally pulling out—like, right now."

"Switch me. NOW."

He was *so* adamant about switching places.

The next short sequence of events is not only the last thing I remember about that day, but it is also the *most* painful memory that I will forever have secreted in my mind.

The convoy was halted before we got going, and Sgt. Williams radioed up to Sgt. Falzone that Julio and I were switching places. We were both qualified and competent in either position, so the switch was within protocol, and no one thought twice about it. I unstrapped my harness, and Julio threw it on and fastened it in over his shoulders. He hopped up into the turret; I took my seat in the back after I locked him in; and we radioed in that we were good to go.

We had been advised from recent intelligence to prepare for probable Taliban activity on the way back to home base. Tucked in between two large canals was the main supply route (MSR) that we were using for our mission back. It was a route that was consistently laced with IEDs and that was known for frequent Taliban activity.

There were several checkpoints manned by Marines with mounted TOW missiles and thermal sites. About a quarter of the way down the MSR, we crossed the first checkpoint. There were no issues that had come about thus far on the mission. But things were not right. The locals were not abiding by their standard daily routines:

- no one was outside working;

- kids weren't chasing our trucks and running alongside of us; and

- other vehicles weren't on the road.

It was quiet.

It was desolate.

We made it to just before the halfway checkpoint, and then it happened. A monstrous blast erupted from below our truck. The boom from the three-hundred-pound command-detonated IED was mind-numbing and was heard for miles.

I blacked out instantly.

JULY 20, 2010

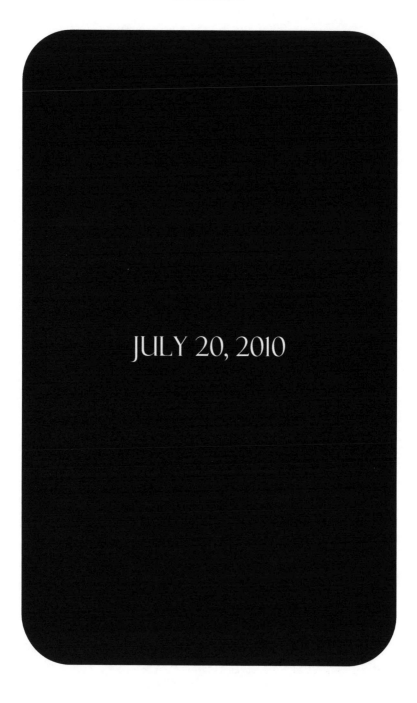

JULY 20, 2010

My team now waged a life-and-death war against time. The next thing I remember is waking up in the hospital in Germany after my surgeries. What I know about that dreadful day and what I am about to share with you is only from what my team has told me.

I was in the back of the vehicle, locked in, and upside-down. My spine was broken in two: the bottom half pierced into my stomach, while the top half tore into my left lung, causing lung failure. My left rib cage was shattered, sending bone fragments throughout my insides. I had a traumatic brain injury from the blast. My chin was ripped open from where my Kevlar® helmet was strapped on.

The convoy of vehicles was stopped immediately as Sgt. Falzone took charge of the chaotic situation. No one could see anything. The massive cloud of dust and debris engulfed everything in its path.

For several seconds, which seemed like hours, there was a hellacious darkness.

The first radio response came in: "FOURTH VIC IS HIT! FOURTH VIC IS HIT!"

As the dust started settling, they could begin to see our fourteen-ton mine-resistant ambush-protected vehicle (MRAP) blown completely over on its topside. The incredible force from the bomb sheered the turret off its bolts and sent it flying about thirty meters from the truck. The rear axles were severed, and the back tires were blown off.

Everyone was thought to be dead.

My driver was the first to crawl out of the wreckage. He was extremely disoriented and didn't know what was going on. He emerged, swearing and yelling for help. Doc Mervau, Lt. Col. Erwin, and Cpl. Galvan immediately dismounted out of the safety of their own vehicle and ran onto the firing grounds to help. They opened their back hatch, and Lt. Col. Erwin told Doc to grab onto the back of his flak jacket and stay close as they blindly finagled their way through the dust and debris to my vehicle. Galvan radioed in to Sgt. Falzone, explaining the situation and telling him that we had one KIA, and that we needed Marines to help evacuate the wounded. Lt. Col. Erwin was the first person to get to me. Cpl. Tunney and Cpl. Frodin extracted Sgt. Williams out of the vehicle. He was assessed, and without hesitation he took his place on forward security, while Doc began trying to find a way into the wreckage to start treating me.

The back doors of the MRAP weren't opening. The metal floor edge was so warped that the doors wouldn't budge.

They called out the need for an emergency medevac helicopter, while several more Marines joined in. They were put on security, setting up a 360 security zone. These Marines were jumping in the deep-watered canal in full gear to set it up.

Back at the MRAP, Doc and Erwin devised a plan to get me out. They could hear me screaming and moaning inside. After clawing at the back door with their bare hands, they took their knives out and started digging out the passenger-side door, which they managed to pry open halfway.

While Doc crawled inside to start getting me out, Galvan was preparing the stretcher. Doc and Erwin had to twist and tug to get me to the door feetfirst.

Galvan, awaiting me at the door, grabbed onto my feet. Erwin grabbed me by the belt and left shoulder, and Doc had my head.

They meticulously twisted my broken, bloodied body around to get me out of the MRAP. Due to the blast, the stretcher that they were going to place me on was broken and would not stay straight. No matter how they positioned it, the stretcher would not properly lock in place. Someone grabbed a secondary stretcher, and it would not straighten out either. They were quickly losing time. Galvan and Erwin tried as hard as they could to get the stretcher to work, but they just couldn't get it. Doc couldn't administer morphine to me, because I had a head injury, so I just lay there in excruciating pain.

My helo was inbound. Cpl. Arceneaux was flawlessly managing communications with the combat operations center while simultaneously keeping up communications with the bird. While awaiting my medevac and keeping perimeter security, my team started taking fire from a nearby compound. Sgt. Falzone knelt beside me and tried to keep me awake. I was dozing in and out of consciousness. He tried to stay as calm as he could so I wouldn't worry. My body was in shock and was quickly shutting down.

He said, "Hey, bud, you're going to be okay, and we're going to get you out of here."

I tried speaking but could barely mumble as spit mixed with blood was popping from my lips.

He again tried reassuring me and said, "A helicopter is on its way."

I mumbled back, "What's a helicopter?"

So he explained in the simplest way what a helicopter was. In the middle of a firestorm, he started making hand gestures and noises like a helicopter to help me understand. He knew that I was out of it, but he just wanted me to be as calm as possible.

Galvan approached Falzone and said, "The medevac will be here in ten mikes [minutes]." At that time he knew that he had to set up some kind of landing zone for the helicopter. He decided on a place on the road behind the safety of the MRAPS. The pilot started getting lower to the road, preparing to land, but the thick dust from the road filled the air. He said over the radio that he could not land there, and he was going to put it down on the other side of the canal.

They gathered every available Marine to help carry me on the jimmied stretcher. Falzone manned the front; Lt. Col. Erwin was on my left; Galvan, the assistant squad leader, was on my right; and Doc had my back. My brothers surrounded me and kept my brittle life safe. Since Falzone was in the front, guiding the litter team to the helicopter, he was looking for the best place to cross the canal.

The canal's wall, going down on the side nearest to the road, was about a four-foot decline. The water spanned only about five feet across but was filled not only with neck-deep water but also with sewage and waste. The wall on the other side of the canal was much larger; it was about seven- to nine-feet high with a gradual incline.

As they walked me down the road in the midst of chaos and enemy fire to find a spot to cross, they decided to cross right where the doors to the helicopter were—where they would load me in. They began to transport me across the water.

Doc had to hand me off to another Marine, because the water was getting too deep. He told me that I was going home, and that everything was going to be okay. Then he posted security as he watched them carry me on.

It took nearly five minutes to cross that water, keeping me up and out of it. I would groan, pass out, wake up screaming and spitting up blood, and then pass over into darkness again.

By the time the Army flight medic received me at the helicopter, I was out cold. My exhausted brothers watched as they loaded me in and carried me off the war-torn battlefield. In a last-ditch effort, shots were fired at the escaping helicopter by the distant terrorists.

A team of Marines that was nearby showed up and took over security for our guys. A wrecking crew and an explosive ordinance disposal (EOD) team arrived to begin cleaning up the devastation left by the bomb.

***

After three hours of grueling combat operations, reality started to slow down. An emotional tidal wave rushed over my brothers as Julio's body was recovered. It was placed under the cover of a blanket and entrusted to the loving care of team three's MRAP. The Marines now became guardians as they silently transported their fallen brother back home.

The rest of our platoon was awaiting their arrival at base. The Marines stood together as one as they said their good-byes and watched as Julio was taken off into the Afghanistan sky in the helicopter. The fight that afternoon to get me off the battlefield was nothing compared to the emotional torment of losing Julio. A memorial service was held that week for Corporal Julio Vargas, honoring his dedication, love, and selfless sacrifice for his family, his Marine Corps, and his beloved country.

Out of respect, a flag was draped over his cot for the duration of the deployment.

***

My brothers were overheated from the burning sun. They were exhausted—physically and mentally. They were in shock after seeing one of their own taken by the hands of the enemy. They were beaten down, but not for a second did they stop and think about themselves. My team, my treasured brothers, gave everything they had that day to get me out of that place; and in doing so, they saved my life. I am forever grateful.

> *My team, my treasured brothers, gave everything they had that day to get me out of that place; and in doing so, they saved my life. I am forever grateful.*

The Army flight medic breathed into me for fifteen consecutive minutes during the flight, because I could no longer breathe on my own with my punctured and collapsed lung. My heart stopped three times while on that fateful helicopter ride to the hospital; but something in me wasn't done fighting. I wasn't ready to go.

My life was far from over.

A wakening from my coma was like trying to claw my way out of the depths of hell. I was coming back to life, but never had I felt more like staying dead.

The first thing you need to understand about this awakening was that the last thing I remembered was being in Afghanistan.

One minute I was conducting a mission in the heart of Marjah, Afghanistan, and with what seemed to be a blink of an eye, I was confined to a bed, with tubes and needles breeching my body and with strangers hovering all around me with white coats draping their bodies and lab masks covering their faces as if I were a deadly disease.

All of this was unraveling in a somber white-walled room in what I *didn't* know was an Air Force hospital, operated out of Landstuhl, Germany. I was convinced upon opening my eyes that I was somehow captured and was now being tortured.

My rapid—and I truly do mean *rapid*—situation-assessment thoughts went something like this:

Where am I?

How do I escape?

Where is my team?

Are they alive?

Are they being tortured?

Am I being tortured?

Who are these people?

How am I going to kill them?

How will I escape?

Phase I – Enemy & Instinct

I opened my eyes, and the first thing I experienced was an invasive tube slithered down my throat, gagging me. A nurse, whom I at first thought to be a terrorist, quickly ran into the room, accompanied by a man in a white lab coat.

My initial reaction was to grab the woman as she reached toward me, isolate and manipulate her outstretched arm, and eliminate the distance between us. With a quick shot from my forearm to her carotid artery, I should be able take her out. She was small.

It has to be fast—no time for mistakes. The well-trained terrorist posing as the American doctor will attack right away. With a quick maneuver off the bed and a short tussle, I should be able to get out of this alive. I see one door and a hallway. In the hallway there are three more doors. They are closed. What's behind them— guards? How many? Guns?—need those. Someone here has guns. Brad, get a weapon. Find your team. Escape.

It was a great thought; however, not only was I entirely too high on multiple drugs, but I also couldn't really move. This became apparent to me when I grabbed at the nurse as she reached for the tube just before I attempted to put her in an arm bar. The harsh reality took over, and it consumed me.

Enter, panic attack:

> *Fite, control yourself! Breathe. Assess.*
> *In...out...in...out.*

My fingers began tapping out a rushed 4/4 tempo, and I began counting.

The woman now feared me. Her eyes were blank and widened; her breathing was shaken, and I could feel her fear as she backed away from me.

> *Brad, why the hell is she backing away? How is she afraid? She's a trained terrorist. She shouldn't be acting like that. That's not right.*

Before I finished processing that thought, the man in the lab coat began to *attempt* to calm me down.

"Bradley...Bradley, you're safe. You're in an American hospital."

My training and thinking were not only louder than his comforting words, but they were faster.

Fite, he's lying! He is a terrorist posing as an American, trying to gain your trust and make you believe that he's on your side! HE'S NOT!

He reassured me: "Bradley, I am a doctor. You've been in an accident. I am here to help you."

My thoughts—an inner battle between my rational self and my survival training—again cut him off:

Fite, you know better than that! He's about to torture you. You know what's going on! Don't let him near you!

But, Training, I think he's trying to take this tube out—and I really want this damn tube out.

Fine, you can let him near you—but just to take out the tube. Then kill him and escape!

I can't escape—remember? MY LEGS DON'T WORK!

The man pulled the tube out of my throat, and I took my first true breath on my own. All I wanted to do was reach out and choke him, but it felt so good to not be gagging on that tube that I just lay my head back and breathed. With a sigh of relief, the man took the tube and exited my room.

It had now been approximately forty-five seconds since I had opened my eyes.

Phase II – This is real...*this is real.*

Though he had helped me with the tube, I still utterly refused to trust the man. I trusted my training, and I knew that I was right about this; however, there was this tiny whisper of a voice coming from somewhere deep inside my head, telling me that I should believe him.

What was this voice?

Where was it coming from?

Was this my fear talking to me?

Was it actual logic, or was it truth?

My training, though, was still overpowering all other thoughts. My brain was still operating in combat mode, and that was not shutting down anytime soon. I would not allow it to. I *could* not allow it to. My life depended on it.

To this point, I did not have the time to properly evaluate logic and reality. The room I was lying in just wouldn't stop moving, and that was incredibly strenuous on my heavily medicated mind. People were continually walking in and out. Strangers seemed to be documenting everything as they watched me through the giant window in the wall of my room. They were staring at me like I was a rare and dangerous animal at the zoo. With every change of my baseline (my natural surrounding), my brain came up with a new and detailed situation report. I was exhausting myself trying to memorize every new face, detail, and sound.

With a satellite phone in hand, the doctor reentered my room. I could sense his nervousness, and I was feeding off of it. I began feeling a sense of pride as I glanced over at the women observing the doctor as he approached my bedside. As they peered through the window, I watched as their faces went from nervous to concerned to frightened. They were afraid of me, which meant that I was doing my job.

Calmly, he spoke to me. "Bradley, I have someone who would like to speak to you."

He was a terrorist, so naturally, I did not reply. I just stared at him while trying to ignore the throbbing pain continuously coursing throughout my body. I could not let him see that I was hurting. He wouldn't get anything out of me—especially not the satisfaction of knowing that I was in pain. My eyes were still and focused, but my mind was racing:

He has a phone.

Who am I about to speak to?

Who do they have?

Do they have my family—how would they?

Okay, stay calm.

Don't speak—just listen.

You can do this.

He handed me the phone, and I slowly put it up to my ear. An alarmingly cheerful voice came on over the wire: "Fite! Hey, Fite—you there? Hey, man, it's Gunny! How are you feeling? Fite—it's me, Gunny!"

On the phone was my platoon sergeant, Gunnery Sergeant Loyola. I knew it was Gunny, and I believed him when he spoke. I couldn't talk. I could hardly breathe. My heart felt like it was breaking into a million pieces as he spoke to me. I felt another panic attack coming on. (I *really* don't like panic attacks.) The truth overwhelmed me. The only thought surfacing after I realized that my injuries were real and that I truly was lying in a hospital bed was regarding the whereabouts of the rest of my team. I lay there in disbelief as I began to muster up the first words that I would speak after waking up:

"Guns, is…is everyone else okay? Are they okay?"

After what seemed to be an eternal pause, my platoon sergeant gathered his composure, and with a shaky yet firm and reassuring tone, he told me that we had lost one. I vaguely remember him instructing me to focus on my recovery, and that everything was going to be okay. I'm sure he said more, but I checked out and stopped listening after he informed me that one was lost.

I knew instantly who we had lost, and the pain of that realization trumped everything else that was going on around me. The realization that one of my greatest friends was no longer alive was an overwhelming pain, unlike anything I have ever experienced. It was worse than not having the use of my legs...worse than the thought of spending my life in a wheelchair...worse than the burning and piercing pain I felt all over my body.

It was a pain that amplified when I grasped the fact that I was going to live, and that I was going to be forced to live every day, knowing that I had killed my best friend. With that singular thought, my mind became my worst enemy and my cruelest critic. The inner battle began, and it would be the greatest fight of my life.

Welcome to reality, kid.

And let me tell you, reality really sucked. I wished more than anything that I could just go back to defense mode, thinking that I was in a terrorist prison camp about to be tortured and killed. Anything was better than this. The thought of living was torture. I did all that I could to *not* think and just to zone everything out.

51

I couldn't. It was the first time in my life that those words, "I can't," came out of my mouth—and the worst part was that I believed it. My self-doubt grew into a giant, and I was in no shape to face a giant.

Phase III – Time

All I had was time, and time was not my friend. Minutes felt like hours, and days felt like years. The only thing on the wall in my room was a small digital clock. I would stare at the seconds as they monotonously changed over from one to the next. I would just lie there, hopelessly, and right when I wouldn't feel alive, the shooting pain in my back would send me a reminder that indeed I was.

I felt pain. I felt utterly helpless. I felt weak. I felt vulnerable. I felt like a dead man living. I felt anger. I felt darkness. I felt a sense of vengeful rage that I somehow had to figure out how to contain inside me. And despite all of those feelings, I felt numb to the core.

I would try to sleep and rest my body and mind, but I would end up just lying motionless in my bed, thinking about the men who did this to me. I thought about the man who hit the button to trigger that fateful bomb. I wondered if he had a family. Did he even have some kids? I would create the most beautiful images in my mind about finding him, torturing his perfect little terrorist family, and killing them all. Every time I would plan it out, I felt like I was composing a grand song and directing the magnificent orchestra playing it. The scene was stunning, but harshly, I would always be brought back to reality.

> *The pain was the only thing letting me know that I was alive.*

Sleep was an interesting dilemma. All I wanted to do was to be able to fall asleep, hoping to escape reality for a little while. Yet, I did all I could do in order to stay awake: I fought sleep. It was a war on two fronts, and it was unclear which one was the bigger fight.

On the one side, I felt obligated to stay awake, because I thought I needed to feel and endure this pain. I convinced myself that I deserved it. My best friend was dead because of me; therefore, I ought to hurt and feel unimaginable pain. My doctor urged me to accept an epidural and told me countless times how much it would help with the pain. I declined it every time. The pain was the only thing letting me know that I was alive.

On the other side, I was dreadfully afraid of the nightmares that I was now cursed with. My nightmares were a dark, inescapable hell. I fought the effect of the medications pulsing their way through my veins and my body's yearning desire to sleep so hard that exhaustion would set in. Eventually— unknowingly—I would slip into sleep. In sleep came death, demons, agonizing pain, and pure darkness. I thought reality was bad, but I swiftly realized that my torturous dreamland was much worse.

I would dream vividly. My dreams felt like real life, and due to my extreme mental exhaustion, it became hard for my strained mind to decipher the difference between dreams and reality. I would sink into panic attacks often, because I thought I was dreaming, when in actuality, I was just lying there awake. The hallucinations became a routine occurrence.

As I watched the clock cross over into the evening hours, a sense of preparation took over. Days were one thing, but nights were an entirely different demon. The agonizing screams and moans of my brothers were the soundtrack to my nights. The hallways echoed with horror and pain. In the room next to mine was also a victim of an IED explosion. Not only was he wrapped up like a mummy from the severe burns, but he was also missing both legs and an arm. I listened to his unceasing suffering and wanted nothing more than to take just an ounce of his pain for him. I did not know his name; I knew him by his screams. His loving wife was there by his side, and I remember the night he found peace.

For a brief period, it was quiet. A haunting somberness seemed to fall over the entire ward. It was like God himself came to our hall to personally escort him to eternity. The halls were silent, and I knew that he had gone to be with his brothers.

The silence was short-lived as the swarming echoes from the weeping of a widow consumed our rooms. The sound of her pain and tears felt like bullets. Her tears seemed to silence all our pain for that moment. It was eerily quiet that night after she left his room. It felt as though all the injured Marines on my ward regained a sense of life, and like the brothers we were, we fought together through that dark night.

We fought the demons.

We fought the pain.

We remembered who we were.

We fought for the brother we lost that night.

We fought for each other.

That night we came together and showed the pain that tormented us that *we* were stronger.

I lay motionless in my bed as I thought of my brothers still fighting in Afghanistan. I thought of my lost friend. I thought of my family. I remembered who I was, and so I prayed. I closed my tired eyes, and I slept peacefully for the first time in weeks.

I opened my eyes the next morning in disbelief that I had actually slept, and I experienced the last thing I was expecting. I felt something weird: I had a tingling sensation all over the lower half of my body. It was my legs.

Somewhere in the course of that night I had regained sensation in my legs, and it wasn't long until I began moving my toes.

The time that followed in Germany became one of my harshest battles, and I am proud to say that it was one of my greatest victories.

My nightmares continued to haunt me while in that white-walled prison, and I had a feeling that they were going to be around for a while. I was semioptimistic that they were just an effect of the harsh narcotics that were operating my mind—but they weren't. The nightmares and pain did not subside, but I found a small sense of hope in the fact that I was moving my toes. Soon I would be transferred back to American soil. So I focused on that.

During my initial days in Germany, I had no feeling or movement from the waist down. I was told that I would be wheelchair-bound, and that due to the amount of metal in my spine, feeling would most likely not return to my legs.

One of the greatest memories I have is the day my doctor walked into my room with a big grin on his face and told me that I was going home. It was the first time I saw him in his full dress uniform, and it was also the moment that I realized that I had cursed at, had spat on, and had plotted to kill a very high-ranking officer in the Navy. (*Nice work, Brad.*) He came over to my bedside, stuck out his hand, and told me that it had been a pleasure getting to know me.

My initial response was to laugh and say, "Yeah, *right*! I was terrible!" But I shook his hand and just began crying. He told me that he had never seen such an array of injuries, and that when I had shown up on his operating table, it was the first time that he had not known where to start. He also let me know that he had done everything possible that he could to give me my body back. As I held onto his hand, with tears streaming down my face, I assured him that he did, and that I *would* make a full recovery—no matter what *anyone* told me.

> I assured him...that I would make a full recovery— no matter what anyone told me.

I have never felt such an assortment of emotions. I was ecstatic, but at the same time, I was still in so much physical pain. I was incredibly eager to leave Germany, but I was so very afraid of what the next hospital would have in store for me.

The nurse came into my room, and he began prepping me for transfer.

This man—unfortunately, I do not remember his name—spent many nights outside my room, because I begged him to be there in case I fell asleep. I begged him to *not* allow me to sleep, and if I *did* fall into a dream, to wake me up. Almost every time I woke from a nightmare, this man was there by my side, reminding me that it was just a dream and reassuring me about where I was. I was proud—*am* proud—to say that there are men and women like that to care for our wounded troops.

I was about to be rolled out of my room, and I asked him to come with me to the plane. He did. I remember, as the team of doctors rolled my bed down the hallway, trying to look into my neighbors' rooms, hoping to get a glance at who they were. I knew their screams but not their faces. I didn't have very much luck; my vision was terribly blurred, and the movement of my bed was making me sick.

We rolled out of the elevator and came to the exit door. The team of doctors stopped at the door and smiled around me, as if they were just taking it all in. I understand it now—why they did that. At least, I think I do: they were excited to see one of their patients living; they were elated to see one of their own have a chance to live again. I can't imagine that they ever got to see their patients after they left that hospital. I came to them nearly dead, and now I was leaving them alive.

They placed a coin on my chest and asked me if I was ready to feel some sunshine. I was. The doors opened, and the lobby of the hospital erupted into applause. I felt like I had just scored the winning touchdown at the Super Bowl, and the crowd was going wild! It was amazing.

An ambulance was waiting for me right outside, and I was loaded up. It happened far too quickly. The second that sun hit my face and I felt the air on my skin, I just wanted to savor that moment. I was loaded into the truck, and the nurse came up with me, shook my hand again, and assured me that I was going to live a great life. He made me promise him that I would never give up, and that no matter what challenge I faced, I would endure it and come out stronger than ever. I took his hand and promised him that I would.

I wish that I could tell you how amazing and relaxing the next fourteen hours on that plane were, but I can't. It was awful. I was the last one loaded into the back of the massive aircraft. My heart broke as I looked in and saw a multitude of Marines strapped into beds just like mine. Many of them appeared in far worse shape than I was in. There were too many for me to count. The sounds echoing in that aircraft will haunt my memories for the rest of my life. The painful moaning, yelling, cussing, screaming, and crying of the afflicted drummed out the noise of the loud engines.

The streaming cocktail of Dilaudid, morphine, and Ambien polluting my brain seemed to not even *touch* my pain. I was strapped in, ready for my flight, and I felt a sense of panic as I lifted my head and watched the back hatch rise to lock us all in. The panic within me was surfacing. It was rising at a rapid rate. I was trapped in again. My thoughts were racing. I was thinking about being locked inside our vehicle that was hit. I was thinking about worst-case scenarios: What if the plane crashed, or what if the terrorists were targeting this plane?

WHY CAN'T MY BRAIN JUST STOP?

I kept begging for more medications. I was calling out for the flight nurse constantly, but so was everyone else. I would doze off—but never more than a couple of minutes. Every time the plane would hit even the slightest turbulence, I would wake up, and an overwhelming sense of nausea would ensue. I threw up on myself, and each time I did, I would lose the medication that was intended to keep me calm.

There was no escaping; all I could do was endure. And endure I did. The flight seemed endless. Over and over again I repeated inwardly: *Tomorrow has to come at some point. Tomorrow has to come at some point.*

One of the nurses began doing something that I thought was strange. She walked around to each individual bed, leaned over, and whispered something to the patient. Suddenly, upon hearing what the nurse had to say, the groaning would stop, and the injured Marine would smile. I wanted to know what she was saying! When was she going to make it to me?

Finally, she came to my bed. She smiled, leaned over me, and said, "Welcome home, hero. We are in America."

> I knew that it was only a matter of minutes now until this aircraft full of the broken brave touched down in the land of the free.

For a second, all my pain dissipated, and I felt nothing but pure joy and relief. I knew that it was only a matter of minutes now until this aircraft full of the broken brave touched down in the land of the free.

A few short minutes later, the pilot came over the intercom and officially welcomed all of us back home. Every five minutes he came back on and gave us an estimated time of arrival. I cannot properly explain to you the excitement and pure ecstasy that I was feeling now. Pain? What pain? I was minutes away from landing in Washington, DC, and I knew that my dad was waiting for me there.

In Afghanistan, we would often joke about what we missed about home and what we were going to do as soon as we got back. Taco Bell binges and strippers were among the top favorites. It is amazing how things change—how one thing can alter your perspective for a lifetime.

All I wanted was to be home. I wanted to be with my family and my friends. I wanted to be alive in America. Knowing that I was minutes away from seeing my dad on American soil was now my painkiller. And it was working.

"Nurses and attendants, please prepare for landing."

We all began yelling and cheering—well, to the best of our ability. There was a corpsman lying next to me. We didn't speak to each other during the flight, but we shared a moment as our plane touched the ground. As everyone began to clap, I looked over at him, and he was lying there with a smile on his face. He looked at me and said, "Trust me. I'm clapping on the inside, brother!" He was missing both his arms just below the shoulder.

It was happening.

A rush of pain swept over my body as we hit the ground and as the plane began shaking my shattered spine around. It hurt like hell, but I didn't even care. I was on American ground, and that was far greater than any pain. I began to cry as the realization that I was finally home began to set in.

I lay there and stared at the back hatch of the plane, awaiting its opening. I was taking steady, deep breaths and was mentally preparing for what was about to happen. And that's when it hit me:

What is about to happen?

I am back home—but what now?

My whole life has changed.

Everything is going to be different. Whoa.

The hatch began to open, and I saw American sunshine shining in on us. It was majestic, and it is one of the most beautiful memories that I have.

I remember inhaling my first breath of American air. I was enjoying it.

I was just lying there taking it all in, and then from the back of the plane, one of the Marines yelled out, "We're home, boys! HOO-RAH!"

Without hesitation, Doc, lying next to me, looked over and said, "Yeah! *I'm* home, but my arms are still in Afghanistan! But hey—I'm pretty sure I got blown up giving them the finger, so now there are two tatted Doc arms forever in that hellhole, saying, '@#$% you, Taliban!'"

It was so good to be home.

I remember landing in Washington, DC, after my long flight from Germany and thinking to myself, "I'm home. No more war."

If I had only known.

For the majority of us, coming home is just the beginning of the war. Our biggest battle is the fight to rejoin society as a "normal" person. Coming home from a war-torn battlefield to a society that will never quite understand is a relentless battle.

For me, everything was different. I spent much of my time in isolation. I not only cut out everyone I loved but turned them into my enemies as well. I didn't go out; all I wanted to do was sit at home in silence and watch TV, but I wouldn't even watch the television. I would just zone out to the mindless noise. Insomnia took over my nights, and if I *did* end up somehow falling asleep, my nightmares drug me into a dreadful world.

I couldn't stand being in crowded places. Everywhere I went, my mind raced with situational awareness. I couldn't even sit at a restaurant without first plotting exit strategies and ranking the top potential threats in the room. I was impulsive. I was hateful. I trusted absolutely no one. I had to relearn how to be a human. It made relearning how to walk look easy.

> I had to relearn how to be a human. It made relearning how to walk look easy.

I was home, but my battle was just getting started. I remember the first time I looked in the mirror and passionately hated the thing looking back at me. There are so many aspects of war that continue on even after we leave the literal combative war zones; and those things change again an already changed man.

I was trained for combat, for survival, to never lose. It didn't matter who or what I was fighting; I would find a way to win. If my enemy was bigger, stronger, or more skilled, I would still triumph. I was never scared to bleed, and the rush of battle excited me. With this confident aggression, I went to war in

Afghanistan to fight Al-Qaida and the terrorists that were threatening freedom. Yet when I came home, my entire fight changed. I was now standing face to face with a new enemy, and it was the one thing I would never want to fight: myself. I was an animal. I was brutal, and I knew it. This fight scared me.

How do I win?

Can I win?

How do I fight something that refuses to lose?

How do I fight something that knows every tactic that I know and plan to use?

I'm fighting me. I'm waging an all-out, bloody-knuckled battle to the death against myself! If I win, a part of me dies, and if I lose, a part of me still dies. Where is the victory in that?

This revelation hit me like a freight train, and it scared me to the core. It was the first time that I actually felt scared about what was to come. Despite my fears, I accepted the challenge, knowing full well that this was going to be the fight of my life.

I constantly found myself getting so frustrated with my life and the endless battling. I wasn't in Afghanistan anymore, so why did I have to keep fighting this damn war?

A friend of mine jokingly said, "Brad, at least there aren't IEDs and suicide bombers here!"

Wrong. There are IEDs, and there are suicide bombers. They have just taken on a new form.

I lost friends—brothers—in Afghanistan, fighting in this war. I saw firsthand the devastating aftermath of bombs and bullets. The thing is, these bombs didn't just explode: they discharged thousands of deadly various forms of shrapnel within their blast.

Here on the home front, we may not have bombs blowing us up in the middle of the road, but we are losing thousands upon thousands of veterans via suicide. That leaves a trail of ruin that charts on an entirely new level. I have lost six of my brothers to suicide, and let me tell you, the wake of destruction that follows their death is just as unbearably painful.

I remember the first time I encountered a brother's suicide. It was hell. It was a catastrophic mental explosion. Emotional shrapnel penetrated to the soul and burrowed its way into every facet of my life. I watched as his family mourned his death and as his friends entered into a state of shock.

In some ways, it's worse here at home. It's an emotional IED and a new form of suicide bombing. When you go to war, you expect suicide bombers, and you expect devastation from IEDs, but it breaks my heart to now expect the same here at home. We are trained to handle those kinds of situations in combat, but you can never be trained to handle losing one of your friends to suicide.

Before deployment, we were sent on a training operation called IED Lane Setup in the hills of Camp Pendleton. The mission of the training exercise was to prepare us to spot possible IEDs. The bombs in Iraq and Afghanistan were masterfully crafted, intricately positioned, and meticulously hidden. The training was to help us learn the most common ways in which the enemy was setting up its deathtraps. Even though we were trained, spotting an IED was still nearly impossible.

Unfortunately, many veterans have mastered this same practice in hiding their real emotions. They have the uncanny ability to take this to an entirely new level with their training in cover and concealment.

> Even though we were trained, spotting an IED was still nearly impossible. Unfortunately, many veterans have mastered this same practice in hiding their real emotions.

As Marine recruits, we heard the terms *cover* and *concealment* until they were drilled into our young, moldable minds. The combat arts of taking cover behind a pile of sandbags or concealing yourself in the tall grass in order to not be hit or seen by the enemy were crucial in the making of young Marines.

Those tools are paramount to survival in combat situations, and that kind of tactical thinking does not go away. They pound it into our being until it becomes instinctual to us. There is no off switch, and it molds the way in which we live, even long after returning home from the combat zone.

It's difficult, sometimes, to be able to tell who the suicidal ones are, mainly because we are so good at concealing our inner feelings and motives. Silence and stealth are among our top qualities when it comes to killing the enemy; unfortunately, they remain the same when it comes to claiming our own lives.

I remember—like it was yesterday—the first time I ever covered my face in camouflage war paint. It was a magnificent transformation from human to warrior, and it was a transformation of not only my skin but my soul; it was spiritual.

My entire mind-set changed with one swoop of paint.

I was in boot camp at Parris Island. We had just set out for the Crucible—the final test before young recruits were given their Eagle, Globe, and Anchor and officially gained the hallowed title: United States Marine. I sat there after just completing the march out to the training grounds, exhausted. From the rear of my platoon, my drill instructor's coarse voice rang out with the command: "War up, recruits!"

I reached down into my perfectly packed bag and pulled out a small field mirror and my war paint. In a design suitable for a warrior, I meticulously applied the greens, blacks, and browns to my face.

I built an entirely new life from behind my mask, and in doing so, I became an extraordinary imposter. I learned to fake everything.

Instantly, with the application of three shades of paint, I became a new person. I was no longer tired. I was no longer sore. Weakness was nowhere to be found. I was a warrior ready to complete the task set before me. The pain and exhaustion were hidden under my warrior's mask.

We—rather, *I*—use that same tactic here, stateside.

I didn't want people to see what was truly going on with me. Yeah, I was scared. I'll admit it. I was scared to death of what I thought would be society's mindless judgment, so I reverted back to my instincts and constructed a mask. I fashioned a covering and daily hid behind its deceitful comfort. I became an artist of the worst sort. I built an entirely new life from behind my mask, and in doing so, I became an extraordinary imposter. I learned to fake everything.

It was exhausting living like that. I was constantly changing masks for different occasions: faking one emotion to cover another. I believed the same lie that so many of us are still falling into today—that it was *not* okay to feel bad sometimes. My life became lie after living lie. I forced myself to bury any emotion that might be considered weak.

I remember the day that I made my mask a part of me and not just a daily accessory.

I was driving to the naval hospital downtown San Diego when the life-changing situation occurred. My drive began at Camp Pendleton, so I had roughly about forty miles to cover. I had made this exact drive many times before, so I knew every exit and every possible detour along the way.

At this mile mark, I have thirty-six minutes left.

At this billboard, I have fourteen minutes until I reach my exit.

Driving was always a bittersweet adventure for me. On one side, the sweet side, I used my time in the car as a time to block out the world around me, crank my music up as loud as it would go, and just lose myself in the music.

On the not-so-sweet side, the reason I would crank my music so loud and try to block out the world was because driving was extremely difficult. Trash on the side of the road became possible IEDs. Overpasses became possible sniper vantage points. Cars became possible vehicle bombs. People walking on the side of the road became possible suicide bombers. Traffic jams became the perfect target and the perfect time for a terrorist to strike. I had a ruthless sensation that I was being followed whenever I was on the road, and I chalked it all up to instinct.

***

I have had an overwhelming fear since arriving back in the States: that the terrorists who blew us up were going to realize that they failed in killing me, and that they were going to come back to finish the job. This fear has single-handedly stopped me from so many things. It is one of the main reasons why I rarely left the house and why I spent my days in isolation for so long. I would try to use my music when I was driving, hoping it would distract me from this very thought. I would try to get so lost in what I was listening to so that I wouldn't have to think about that one black suburban ten cars behind me that I was certain *had* to be following me.

***

Back to the story:

I was on the highway heading south on an absolutely gorgeous Southern California day. My windows were down, my music was blaring, and I was trying my hardest not to think about all the potential dangers of being on the road. I was about to hit my halfway checkpoint, when a black SUV—the one that I had been keeping an eye on for the past five miles since it had merged its way onto the highway—neared me.

[Mental snapshot of the truck and the exit marker at which it arrived on the highway.]

As I mentioned previously, I was always very aware of my surroundings and made it a point to take mental snapshots of everything that I thought was out of the ordinary—just in case. Well, apparently, going the speed limit in the far left lane was not acceptable to the driver of this vehicle. The SUV got closer and closer to me, and my heart began to race. I noticed the California license plate.

[Mental snapshot of the license plate number.]

The driver of the SUV started showcasing his unhappiness with my speed in a typical road-rage fashion. Let me just tell you, if extreme tailgating were a sport, this guy could have gone pro and would have been the highest-paid athlete.

This went on for miles. I took my eyes off of his vehicle for a split second as I began to get over into the nearest lane to my right. As I tried to make my way over, he whipped his SUV into the next lane, and we almost collided.

It was in that moment when everything began making an extreme transformation. I couldn't fight it anymore. Reality was too real. I knew that it had to be a terrorist operating this SUV, and he was after me.

I accelerated.

80 mph.

SUV stayed on me.

85 mph.

Right on me. I was weaving through traffic like I was racing at Talladega.

90 mph.

He stayed right on me. The black graveled highway turned into rocky desert terrain.

100 mph.

I started to pull away and create some distance.

My supercharged Dodge Charger's engine was roaring.

I looked in my mirror. He was still in pursuit.

I hit some traffic that I simply could not weave my way through at high speed. I was forced to slow down.

He was gaining on me.

I didn't know what was racing faster—my heart or my overworking engine. I was covered in sweat. My hands were gripped to the steering wheel as if I were holding on for dear life. My arms were red from blood vessels that had burst. My eyes were burning from the sweat dripping into them, but I wouldn't take my hands off the wheel to wipe it away.

I pulled off onto the shoulder of the road in order to pass the other cars, and I stepped harder on the gas pedal.

75...80...90...100...110....

I finally made it to my exit, and my tires burned a pungent trail of black smoke as I ripped through a red light and rounded the sharp left corner at the end of the off ramp.

I paid attention to nothing except my rearview mirror, panning the road behind me in search of the terrorist. I approached the gate of the naval base and screeched to a stop.

> *Little did I know that control was something I had lost many, many miles ago.*

Without hesitation, I began briefing the guard about the current situation. I reported to him that there was a black SUV carrying a bomb and operated by a terrorist in current pursuit of me. In one breath I tried giving him every detail that had occurred over the last twenty miles. I could barely breathe anymore. I felt like my heart was going to combust.

I was shaking and trying my hardest to keep control. Little did I know that control was something I had lost many, many miles ago.

Four more guards and a couple of California Highway Patrol officers now accompanied the man at my window. They had me pull over just inside the gate.

I pulled over and began to exit my vehicle in order to help them prepare for the oncoming attack. Before I could step out, a CHP officer—a former Marine with a tour of duty in Fallujah, Iraq—met me and had me sit back down in my car. He asked me to explain the situation to him again, and I began choking on my own breaths. I felt like the entire world was closing in on me, and the harder I tried to stop it, the worse it got. The officer kept talking to me, but his voice sounded like it was coming from miles away. A piercing ringing in my ears began to disrupt my focus.

Darkness.

I opened my eyes, and I was lying in an emergency room. Medics, nurses, and police officers surrounded me. There were two California Highway Patrol officers talking to my wife and the Marine Corps liaison that now accompanied her. In an attempt to calm me down, the doctors had medication flowing through me via an IV. I woke up from my blackout drowsy and confused.

I was desperately trying to piece together what had just happened.

My wife (I'll tell you more about her later) came to my bedside and told me to just be honest with the doctors about what had happened; so I was.

I told them every single detail of the event, and in doing so, I also began to realize that what I had experienced was not entirely real. Don't get me wrong, what had happened was extremely real, but my mind had skewed the truth.

Reality and misconception blended into an extremely blurred line.

I realized that I had experienced a flashback, and that the incident on the road with the SUV was not actually an attempted terrorist attack.

I will never forget the feeling I had when I told the doctors surrounding me again and again what happened and having them respond to me like I was crazy. The nurses looked at me as if I belonged in a mental ward.

And that's exactly where they sent me.

I spent the next two days locked up in a secured glass room with fifteen other patients. My roommate in this glass prison was a kid who could see and communicate with dragons, and they were, together, plotting the demise of earth. The entire ward was on constant suicide watch, which meant that the lights were never turned off. This place was a new form of hell for me.

I was not allowed any contact with the outside world, and I was forced to spend my days in isolation, reflecting on my craziness. My clothes were taken from me, and I now wore a hospital gown labeled: "Property of Mental Health." I began to question everything.

Am I crazy?

Yes, you are.

Is this where I belong?

Well, you're here, aren't you?

Is this what happens when I choose to be honest about my PTSD?

You should've just lied.

If this is how I will be treated, then the world cannot know.

It was in this moment that I began molding my new and improved mask.

I was released from the hospital, and as I walked out those doors, I locked my new mask in place. I fashioned this mask to never come off, and for three years, it never did. It became so much a part of me that I forgot I even had it on. It was my identity. I learned how to fake everything from behind its deceitful disguise. My entire existence became a lie. And that lie took me down a treacherous path.

I could fool those around me, but I couldn't fool myself. I knew the truth, and it was a grueling struggle to hide it.

I was getting good at wearing my new disguise—almost too good. It seemed like life was...well...good.

I started going out more. I once again made time to hang out with friends. I got involved with a youth mentoring program. I was going to church again, and I actually became an active member. My marriage seemed to take a turn for the better, and my relationships were slowly being restored. I mentored younger Marines in my battalion and was even promoted. This "good behavior" went on for months.

Lies.

Lies.

Lies.

And more lies.

I could fake a smile and laughter.

I could fake happiness.

I could fake love.

Wait—I'm lying again. I couldn't fake my way

through love; no matter how hard I tried. I had far too much hate and fear inside of me for that. It is absolutely impossible for love to exist where fear and hate are present; and I was filled to the brim with both.

> *It is absolutely impossible for love to exist where fear and hate are present; and I was filled to the brim with both.*

In war, you see the absolute worst in humanity. You get the haunting privilege of witnessing firsthand the utter depravity of mankind: fathers sell their innocent daughters to ruthless predatorial monsters for nothing more than mere pennies and send their sons off to inevitable death via terrorist training camps. Boys as young as seven years old are forced to strap on explosive vests, with the promise of terroristic salvation in an eternally glorified afterlife. Men and women alike viciously plot ultimate death and destruction in the hailed name of Jihad.

A murderous delusion of holiness unleashes the animal inside of humanity in this unholy war in which we are waged. Trust? How do you trust anything after being exposed to such things? My faith in mankind was lost. I came home and thought that all people were innately evil and incapable of anything good. I trusted no one for this very reason.

Was my reasoning wrong? No. No it wasn't. It's sad, really, but it was justified—to me. Very few people around me truly understood this dilemma.

I thought the only person I could trust was myself, but at that time, that was just another lie. I told myself to trust my instinct, but my instinct wasn't instinct at all—it was just fear. I lived—fearful of living. I was afraid of what I was becoming, and I was scared to death about the future. Was I becoming one of the monsters I so viciously hated? Was I any different from the men I had so eagerly hunted?

I forced myself to push on, even if that meant faking it. Faking it worked for a while, but living a lie was a tormenting battle that exhausted every fiber of my being.

If I were to have any chance of survival from this point on, I had to make my way to the crux of my pain. I couldn't go on lying anymore.

Losing Julio was a deep wound. It was left buried and untreated for years. That singular wound infected the brightest part of my soul and carried me hopelessly into the pits of depression. It was greater than the sum of all my physical injuries. A broken spine was nothing in comparison.

I could—and would—heal from my physical array of injuries; it would just take time. Regarding my physical recovery, I was able to see the end game and the big picture. My doctors gave me timelines, and I created my own timelines from those. I could see daily improvements.

At least once a day I received an "encouraging" message from someone, and somewhere in at least one of the paragraphs, the note, e-mail, or letter would say something along the lines of: "Time heals all wounds." I didn't need time. If anything, I was discovering that time was indeed no friend of mine.

Time meant continuing on, and that was not something that I wanted—nor did I have any idea how to do it.

I catatonically existed as if I had a life sentence in a very dark, isolated prison. It wasn't long until I arrived at a point where I felt like I just could not do it anymore. My so-called *life* no longer mattered to me, especially if it was going to be like this. I couldn't see past the agony. I couldn't function through what I interpreted as limitless defeat.

There was an impenetrable wall constructed from the perfect blend of hate, pain, and self-pity in front of me; and I couldn't figure out how to get over it. I was certain there was no way around it, and I knew that I wasn't capable of powering through it. Those lies left me with only one option: give up—stop trying. So I did. Well, I tried. I attempted to kill myself more than once. The thought of suicide had actually been among the very first in my head upon waking up from my coma.

BRAD C. FITE

My first attempt to selfishly end my life happened just days into my stay in Landstuhl, Germany. I was hurting—hurting not only in my damaged body but also in my heart. I was beaten down and left practically lifeless—but fully broken. The shallow thump appearing on the monitor to my left was proof that my heart was still beating, but I, the withering pile of reconstructed bones stapled up in a swollen sack of flesh, was proof that it was not producing any form of life. I would stare at my heart monitor as if it were my death sentence. I would doze off into scenic daydreams and imagine it flatlining (depression's high-definition entertainment at its finest). I was among peers on that ward—but still somehow so alone. Their painful groans were so close, but their souls seemed so far away. All I had was my darkened and illogical imagination. The endlessly streaming cocktail of medications dulling my senses brought on terrifying hallucinations that became a perpetual occurrence.

My mind was a powerful and dangerous weapon. It may have been in a weakened state, but it wasn't any less dangerous. It fabricated images out of my deepest fears and projected them in convincing actuality. One night, in particular, I saw a man. No, I saw *the man*. He was the terrorist that triggered the IED that blew up my team. He was dressed in a muddy sun-battered man-dress with a tattered headscarf. He still had the trigger in his dirty hands. Blood stained his unmanicured fingernails, and the pungent smell of fertilizer and manure plagued my room. I screamed curses and threats at him. I tried to get up to kill him, but I couldn't move my legs. It was in this heightened moment of self-deceit that I crumbled.

I couldn't take it anymore! I was so overwhelmed with guilt and misplaced anger that I snapped, and the battle within engaged. The tactical voice was screaming in my head:

Julio should be alive.

You stole his life.

I should be dead.

So die.

But I can't do it.

You can do it.

I won't do it!

You will.

More than anything I wanted to see my friend again. I wanted to hug him and feel his presence. I wanted to tell him that I was so, so sorry. I wanted to hear him sing a terribly off-key version of "Chicken Fried" again. I wanted to know that he was in a better place, and I wanted to be with him wherever that place was.

I didn't want to be paralyzed. I didn't want to be in a wheelchair the rest of my life. I didn't want to be sad, angry, and in pain; but really, I didn't want to be afraid anymore. I wasn't used to being afraid. This was a new feeling for me, and it was terrifying.

I assessed my surroundings and took an account of what was available to me, which wasn't much. My conclusion was one that was irrational—but despairingly possible. I would strangle myself, and I would do so with my catheter. Without a second thought, I began the deadly process.

My arms were heavy, but my mission-intent hands were steady. I reached down and gripped the catheter, and on a perfectly timed, full exhale, I quickly yanked it out of my body. I ran the catheter meticulously through my hospital gown to dry it off so that it wouldn't slip out of my clammy grip. I knew that it shouldn't take very long. There was no mental preparation or pep talk needed. My killer, purpose-driven hands were solid and still. My obstinate mind was set. I had my mission, and the mission always came first. My twisted sense of honor assured me that I was doing the right thing.

I had my window for strike.

Do it.

Now!

I was silent. I was deadly. I was ready.

With my goal in mind, I tightly wrapped the catheter around my swollen knuckles, and with all the strength I could muster, I wrapped the death tool around my neck and began to choke the life out of myself.

Fortunately, I was entirely too medicated to coherently and properly execute what I thought was the perfect plan. I do not remember passing out, but I *do* remember waking up.

I was expecting to awaken in a new, bright, and beautiful world with my incredible friend standing there, glowing with happiness in the distance, with his typical whopping grin welcoming me in. I would have no pain. I would have full use of my body. I would be happy. Who knows, I might even be able to fly—that'd be rad!

I was not prepared for my rude awakening.

My heavy, burning eyes opened slowly, and after a few deep breaths, I found myself slouched the exact same miserable way, in the exact same depressing situation, in the exact same dark room. Only now I was covered in and smelled like piss. Oh, and I had a really, really sore neck and a hell of a headache. I put my hand on my chest and cried as I felt the pathetic thumping of my heart—real proof that I was still present in this world. It didn't take long for my deceptive mind to once again capture the situation.

Brad, you can't even kill yourself!

I know...

How useless are you?

So useless...

You don't deserve to live.

I KNOW! But I can't even die...

You are worthless.

I am utterly worthless....

I was drowning in my own despair, sinking deeper and deeper into the vast, mysterious black hole that was depression. My world was spiraling out of control; and control was the one thing I felt like I absolutely needed.

Taking my life was the only thing I felt like I could have control over, and now, I couldn't even do that.

I hated failure. I was the kind of person who, more than anything, hated failing. The mere idea of it was sickening. Even growing up, I was a kid that hated losing: whether it was kickball, dodgeball, or whatever other game we were playing in gym class—all the way up to varsity sporting events. Losing wasn't an option. I wouldn't accept it.

Taking my own life became more than just escaping pain; it became an unyielding game that I felt obligated to win.

I was determined to try again and again until I was victorious.

My second attempt came just a couple short months later, while I was in Bethesda Naval Hospital, Maryland.

Bethesda was its own devilish beast, but one thing remained the same: I was isolated in a small white room that was laced with the invisible blood-soaked tragedy of the men who previously lay there. I blindly ignored every silver lining that was right in front of me every day.

Why couldn't I just be happy to be alive? Why couldn't I find peace in knowing that my friend loved me so much that he laid down his life for mine? Why couldn't I be happy that my family was there and loved me so much? Why couldn't I look at my brothers who were missing their limbs and just be content with my scarred body?

My family made weekly trips from Detroit to Bethesda, Maryland, thanks to the wonderful Semper Fi Fund and the Fisher House. I remember being especially excited for one weekend in particular. My best friend, Barry, was coming to visit me.

Barry and I met in college during an internship in Washington, DC, and we had been inseparable ever since. We were roommates and instantly best friends. After our internship, he moved back to North Carolina, and I headed back to Michigan and began on my road to the military. We stayed very close, and our friendship grew into brotherhood.

Barry is the kind of friend you get once in a lifetime: no matter what, through thick and thin, he's there. And now, when I needed a friend the most, he was on his way.

It was really difficult to find things to be excited about while in the hospital. The normal things consisted of:

> "Dude! My surgery to take off my dead foot is tomorrow! FINALLY! Hell yeah!"

> "Dude! I found a way to get extra morphine! You gotta check it out!"

> "Dude! Have you met the new physical therapist? She's smokin' hot!"

The weekend came, and my family was finally there. Long before the sun came up, my parents moseyed into my room with the daily norm: McDonalds orange juice and oatmeal. My eight-year-old little brother made himself right at home and lounged in the recliner next to my bed, where he played his Nintendo DS religiously.

They were all sitting in my room, wearing their mandatory yellow gowns, when my dad put his hands on my shoulder. It all began as he said, "I'm going to go out and get Barry. He's here, bud."

I was more than excited and so ready to have some bro time.

My dad stood out in the hallway and updated Barry on my condition. They chatted for a while; I could hear their voices, but I couldn't understand what they were saying.

In they walked. Barry came over and gave me a strong hug, and I engaged all the strength I could muster and hugged him back. I wanted him to see that I was still strong. So I tried giving an extra-solid hug.

I started picking up on strange emotions hovering in the room. Something wasn't right. Everyone was getting quiet and just looking at me with sadness in their eyes. I thought it was so weird.

Boz is here; this is supposed to be awesome!

My dad stood behind my bed and started waving everyone out of the room. The doctor closed his notes, told me he would be back later to check in on me, and left with the nurse. My mom and little brother walked out next, and then I watched my dad give Barry a nod as he turned to leave. Before he closed the door behind him, he let me know that they were going to be right outside, and that they loved me very much.

Across the room, I had a new computer that was donated to me from the hospital. But I was never allowed to use it. I also had a new smartphone, but I wasn't allowed to use that either. So many times I tried getting on my computer, because I wanted to check Facebook. I was told originally that it was national security, and that I wasn't allowed to be on social media this soon after the deployment. I was high, so obviously it made sense. I was about to find out the real reason why. It was about to all make sense.

My room was cleared. Just Barry, with his hands in his pockets, was left standing up against the window by my bed.

"This sucks, huh?" I began.

"Yeah, bro, it's pretty bad. But...uh...I actually have some more bad news that I have to tell you."

I was confused. I just said, "Okay."

Barry continued, "So, um...so, the same day that you got blown up over there...Woody was...um...Woody was in a car accident.

"But he's okay, right?"

"They," he hesitated, "they actually found his body a few days later. He was killed, bro."

It didn't make any sense.

There is no way that's true.

I didn't believe him. I kept looking at the door, thinking that he was playing a joke, and that Woody was actually outside the door, waiting to surprise me.

I told Barry to shut up and stop messing with me.

He told me again.

He wasn't kidding.

He told me again.

Still wasn't kidding.

I began screaming, and as the nurses tried to come into my room, Dad stood in front of the door and assured them that I was okay. He knew what Barry was here to do. He knew that Barry was the best person to tell me this horrible news. It had to be done quickly so that I didn't find out via Facebook.

I was so angry!

This is not possible.

This CANNOT be happening right now!

Matthew Wood was a dear, dear friend to us. I had met Matt ("Woody") through Barry in college. Woody was the last friend I saw before I left for Afghanistan. He drove up from Pennsylvania for the

> *My broken heart became a shattered heart, and my fading soul just dissipated into nothingness.*

weekend to party it up one last time before I deployed. We both had huge plans coming to life: I was going to Afghanistan, and he was off to medical school in the Caribbean. *Sun, sand, and señoritas* was the plan for when I got back. He came to Michigan and stayed at my house for the weekend. We went to a Taylor Swift concert; because, what else would two best buds do before massive life-changing events were about to happen? Not even going to lie—it was amazing. It was hands down one of the greatest memories of my life.

Matthew Phillip Wood was killed in a car accident in Pennsylvania the same day that I was blown up in Afghanistan. My broken heart became a shattered heart, and my fading soul just dissipated into nothingness. I am forever grateful for Barry and his willingness to come and be the bearer of bad news. I wouldn't have been able to handle that news without him there. We cried together for a while, and then my parents came in and sat with me while I cried some more.

For the next two weeks, Barry and my dad traded night shifts, sleeping on the reclining chair in my room.

After my family and Barry had gone, I knew more than ever that it was time for *me* to go. This world was not where I wanted to be. I couldn't take any more loss.

First, I had lost my body, and then I had lost my friend. It was time to complete the progression and finally lose my life.

I didn't want to hurt anymore. I simply could not take any more pain or bad news. I couldn't lie on that sticky plastic bed and piss in a bedpan one more day. I needed to be with my friends. I needed to be free of this insufferable pain.

That night I focused. I again assessed my situation and twisted together a murderous plot. My polluted and inexplicably irrational mind spoke beautiful lies:

This time has to be different, Brad.

I know...

Failure is not an option!

I KNOW!

Do you?

YES! Leave me alone!

Well, then prove it....

I knew that I was on blood thinners, and that if I could only find a way to pierce my skin just right, I could bleed out.

I'll use my IV. It's sharp enough.

The lights went out, and the nurses were trading shifts. It was time. It was *my* time.

With a purposeful mind, steady hands, and a calm heart, I pulled out my IV. The steady, cold stream of blood slowly washed down my pale arm. I smiled in relief as I watched the blood paint my skin. I was captivated as I lost myself for a short few seconds in the blood bath. I came back to reality and knew I had to push on. Buzzers and alarms started ringing in my room. I tuned them out. I drove the needle into my wrist. I knew that the nurse would be in shortly, so I had to act fast.

Steady, Brad. Smooth is fast.

I plunged the needle deeper into my vein, and with vile determination I drove it up my arm. I closed my eyes and awaited my sure death. I entered into a state of euphoria as I felt my head get light.

I couldn't live. And now I couldn't even die. I would spend the greater part of the next three years in this limbo. My heart may have been beating, but my spirit was dead.

I n October 2010, only two days after my third failed suicide attempt, at the Polytrauma Unit in Richmond, VA, my world was rocked. I was lying on my plastic-sheeted bed after a grueling physical therapy session in the pool, when an older, white-haired man poked his head into my hate-filled room.

With an uncomfortably cheerful tone, he said, "Hey! How's it goin' in here?"

I opened my tired eyes and turned my head in disgust, ready to fire off one of my standard expletive-laced responses, when I saw what he was carrying. He held two guitars: one strapped over his shoulder; the other, hanging in his left hand. He continued before I even had a chance to spout out a witty comment about his unwelcome presence in my doorway.

"Do you play?"

With a sigh of relief, and a bit of confusion, I replied, "Yes."

"Wanna jam?"

I mumbled out an uneasy, "Sure."

"Well, can I come in?" I nodded, and he eagerly approached my bedside.

Let me interject, briefly, and tell you that I grew up playing music. It started in the second grade when I asked my parents if I could get a violin. Despite what that meant for their ears, they said yes. I had private lessons from my wonderful teacher, Kay Thomas, once a week after school, and that eventually led me into playing in the orchestra all throughout my high school term. As an eighth grader, I began playing the guitar and later began experimenting with the piano. Music always came easy to me. I loved it from the start. No matter what was going on or what I was going through, music was always a constant companion. It was an integral part of my life, especially while I was in the Marine Corps. No matter where I went, my music went with me.

The man, still nameless, pulled over a chair and sat next to my bed. He whipped an older, slightly beat-up guitar off his shoulder and handed it over to me. I was still utterly confused by who this random "old dude" was, and why he was at the hospital, but I didn't really seem to care. I just wanted to play that guitar. I felt like a kid on Christmas morning, about to open the one gift that I wanted more than anything.

One of the tuning pegs was broken, so it was slightly off-key, with little to no hope of it ever truly being in tune. It had some wear-and-tear on its body, but it was the most beautiful guitar that I had ever seen. The man sat there and looked at me, as if he was just waiting for me to strum my first chord and initiate our jam session. I ran my hand down the neck of the guitar, felt the draw of the phosphor bronze strings on my fingers, and couldn't help but smile. I arranged my hand on the fret board and rang out a simple G chord. I felt the vibration of that sound from my ears down to the core of my bones.

One note loosened the noose of depression that was suffocating the life out of me. Six strings and an improvised paper pick made me forget, for that short period of time, how much I was hurting.

We sat together for hours. We never even really spoke or had any form of conversation. We just played music. At the end, the man looked down at his watch and said, "Well, It was a pleasure making music with you, Warrior. The wife's got a hot dinner goin' cold on me, so I gotta run."

He got up from his chair, slung his guitar over his shoulder, and started heading toward the door.

"Sir...your guitar." I held up his other guitar to show him the one I was still holding.

"Yeah? What about it?"

"Well, I kinda still have it."

Without hesitation, he turned around and said, "Kid, that guitar hasn't been played like that in decades; he belongs with you. I'll be back another time. For now, you take care of him for me."

He turned to leave, but he paused and said, "One more thing. That guitar is a great listener. He knows my deepest secrets. You should talk to him."

With that said, he rolled back his shoulders, puffed out his chest, straightened his back, and saluted me.

Before I even had a chance to thank him for his time and his guitar, he was gone. I got in my wheelchair every day after that and rolled around the hospital hoping to find him. I started asking the nurses on my floor and random people outside, where he said he sat and played, and no one knew of this man. The nurses looked at me like I was crazy, because no man with guitars ever checked into our ward (guests always had to check in at the front desk before they were allowed to come back to where our rooms were).

That evening I lay in my bed and wrote my first song, "Dead Man."

I feel like I'm a dead man,
But I'm talkin'.
They say that I'm a dead man,
But I'm walkin'.
I might be a dead man,
But I'm singin' this song.
I look into the mirror, and I see a ghost:
A hollow shadow starin' right back at me.
Medals and scars, a guitar, and some bars
Keep this dead man livin' today.
Alive I was one man;
Now I'm an army.
Lost those chains;

Now no one can stop me.
Bottles and pills, rock, and cheap thrills
Keep this dead man singin' today.

God, if you can hear me,
Keep me talkin'.
God, if you can hear me,
Keep me walkin'.
God, if you can hear me,
Keep me singin' this song.
God, if you can hear me,
Keep me rockin'.
God, if you can hear me,
Keep me rollin'.
Oh, God, if you can hear me,
Keep me singin' this song.

Little did I know then that writing that song would place me directly on a course toward finding the purpose that would someday become my dream, turned career—but more about that later.

That guitar changed my world. Life slowly began making an appearance in me. The darkness wasn't as dark, and the pain didn't seem to be as bad anymore. When I was having a bad day, I sat there and played heavy rock music or wrote bluesy riffs, and if I was having a good day, well, I played happy music.

Music became my therapy. It was healing me, down to my soul.

I was still not able to talk to therapists about what was transpiring in my head, and I felt like a crazy science experiment every time I was forced to go to a psychiatrist. I was making an incredible physical recovery, but mentally, I wasn't making any progress; if anything, I was getting worse. Music started to change that for me. I spoke to my guitar, and it rang out what I had to say in the most beautiful language ever written.

I kept a journal in Afghanistan. I wrote in it every single day. It helped not only pass the time over there, but it also helped me escape reality for a short time. I wrote about everything.

One day I came back to my room from physical therapy, and sitting in my room was a massive box with packaging stickers from Afghanistan. Inside was all my combat gear, some notes from my guys, and my journals. I opened up the box, and dust and sand from Afghanistan flew into the air. All my uniforms, my extra boots, my shattered iPod, my Chicago Bears flag, and my journals—all covered in the stench and dust of Afghanistan.

I pulled out my journals, wiped the dust off, and opened one of them. I began reading, and as I read, I began shaking. Shaking turned into seizing, and then my room morphed into a desert camp with swells of dust and sand. The sounds of war echoing deep from within my brain were projected outward into a twisted reality. There was a bloodied casualty of war on her knees pleading for me to help her. Bombs were exploding, and then I woke up, heart racing. I was slouched in my wheelchair, with my nurse, Beth, kneeling in front of me, holding my hands, reassuring me that everything was just fine.

I was so confused by what had just happened.

What the hell did I just experience?

It had been a flashback.

Before experiencing them myself, I had no idea that kind of thing actually happened to people, and I *never* thought it would *ever* happen to me.

This was only one of many through the years.

That night, when my nurse came in to check on me, she asked me how I was doing and asked if I wanted to talk about what had happened earlier. I was still pretty embarrassed about the whole thing. She told me that I shouldn't feel bad about it, nor should I be scared; it was normal. She set a brand new journal on my bed and said that I should write about good things in this one. So I did.

I started journaling again, and those journals turned into songs. I would sit there in my room and just write and write and write—and then put that writing to music. I was releasing stashes of buried emotions from deep inside my head and heart out into my songs. I actually started feeling better, and I wanted to share it.

I wheeled down to my neighbor's house (room) and started teaching him how to play. Eventually, I was teaching music to three guys on my floor.

Music became something so much larger than just playing instruments: for us, it was healing. It was an escape from our physical pain and the mental torment of PTSD.

There was one Marine, Sergeant Cody. While on his third tour of duty, an improvised explosive device also hit *his* truck, but he and his team weren't as fortunate as mine. The rest of his team was killed, and he was left paralyzed, was fed through tubes, and was isolated to living in a chair. (He is an incredible Marine, and after getting to know his family, I know that he is an even better man.) Though he did not have much use of his body, his mind was still there. I would sit and talk to him, and he'd look me in the eyes the whole time. I started taking my guitar out to play for him. Sergeant Cody was unable to do anything on his own: every day he was fed, bathed, clothed, and watched over by another person. It was time to give him something that *he* could do.

I wanted Sergeant Cody to play music with me, so I downloaded an application on my iPad that allowed the user to play a virtual piano. I enlarged the app so big that there were only four keys on the screen. I wheeled out of my room with my guitar and the iPad and headed straight for Cody. I placed the iPad on the tray of his wheelchair and set his hand on top of it. Sgt. Cody could move his right hand, but his movements weren't really controlled.

"Hey brother, you wanna play some music with me? I brought a piano; it's sitting right under your fingers. Can you touch it?" Cody was able to rest his finger on one of the enlarged notes, and he twitch-tapped a semiconsistent *C* note. I started playing my guitar, and we jammed together. In mere moments, he had "the look" back in his eyes. No one was doing that for him! *He was playing. He was hitting that note!*

I went back to my room that night and wrote down in my new journal what had just happened, and that led to writing out a business plan. I saw firsthand what music could do in a hurting world. I had experienced the healing power of music, and I wanted to share that.

I created Warriors Song, a nonprofit foundation teaching music therapy to combat-wounded veterans. The idea is simple: provide a therapeutic outlet to combat-wounded veterans through the healing influence of music and writing. I love teaching these brave men and women how to release emotions that they are submerging in their heads. These thoughts flow out onto paper, transposing their emotional outpouring of words into lyrics, and then I show them how to play whatever instrument they want to learn. Warriors Song is not advertised as therapy. Going through years of recovery, I strayed away from anything and everything that was labeled as *therapy*. I hated feeling like I was a lab experiment.

Warriors Song is simply about a combat-wounded veteran who used music to crawl out of his depressing black hole, teaching other vets how to do the same. What works for me may not work for others, and that is perfectly fine; however, maybe what works for me *will* work for someone else.

If Warriors Song successfully helps just one veteran find life again, then I consider it a massive success. I wrote out my dreams for the foundation in the journal, and with those words, I expressed what I wanted it to become.

The remainder of my stay in Richmond was not easy, by any means, but it was easier now that I had found a semblance of purpose. I played that beaten-up guitar until my fingers ached. When I started feeling down about life, I wrote a song about it. When I was in pain, I played music to get my mind off of it. Music became my voice throughout recovery, and I realized that sometimes the best words you can say are not spoken—but played.

Through all the chaos that happened in that hospital, somehow a sweet redheaded girl made her way into my whirlwind of a life. Her name was Aimee, and she was a mutual friend of a friend from my days attending college at Liberty University in Lynchburg, Virginia. Because she was close to my best friend, she had been following my story and my recovery. I had met her one time about two years previous to all of this, and because of that one meeting, she and I had become friends on Facebook.

One day after physical therapy I was lying in my bed and grabbed my computer to zone out and do some Facebooking. I had received messages almost nonstop from people, letting me know that they were thinking about me and wondering how life was. I never felt the need to respond to them—mainly because I was a miserable person, and I hated hearing people's various positive outlooks on *my* life.

Aimee sent me a message, letting me know that she was thinking about me and praying for me and asking me to let her know if I ever needed anything.

She was smokin' hot, single (I hoped), and still living somewhat in the area.

I decided I needed something.

I sent her a very simple and blunt message. I asked her if she was single. She responded with a yes, and I then asked her if she wanted to come to Richmond and hang out with me for a day. After a few more messages of subtle urging from my end, she agreed, and the next day she drove the two and a half hours from Lynchburg to Richmond.

I wasn't looking for a relationship, but when she walked into my depressing hospital room and pinned a handmade get-well poster on my wall, I fell in love. She glowed. She was the most beautiful person I had ever seen, and I knew that I was going to marry her.

We spent the day together in my room, talking and eventually watching a movie together. She sat in a chair beside my bed, talking through the whole movie about why I should be "team Edward" and explaining to me why the *Twilight* saga mattered. I fell asleep after my drugs kicked in, and within hours of meeting me, she experienced firsthand the hell that was my nightmares. I began screaming, and the nurses rushed in. I awoke, and when I figured out what had happened, I expected Aimee to run and never return. Instead, she smiled, and in her eyes I felt love. She returned the next day, and the next, and the next. We began dating, even though our relationship consisted of dates down to the chow hall and wheelchair rides through the hospital. She loved me relentlessly from the first day, and I tried as hard as I could to give her the same love in return.

I came to Richmond, Virginia, bound to a wheelchair, with little use of my legs. I was deep in my depression and lost, feeling like I had no purpose in life. In late November, I received my discharge paperwork and walked, with only the aid of two arm crutches and Aimee, out the front door of that hospital. I left with hope for a bright future and an idea that I was determined to make a reality.

Aimee and I continued dating, and on November 23, with a little help from the band *Train* and live on a Detroit radio station, I asked her to marry me. We didn't want to wait, and on December 23, we went downtown Detroit and exchanged vows, beginning our lives together as one.

I returned to San Diego, California, and checked in at Wounded Warrior Battalion West, on Marine Corps Base Camp Pendleton. It took me a while to adjust to being a patient and not a combat-ready Marine.

My days were filled with medical appointments instead of field ops. I went to physical therapy and rode a water bike instead of going to the gym and lifting weights. I was submerged in medical paperwork preparing me for retirement instead of getting my reenlistment documents ready. Life was completely different now, and I was struggling, trying to figure it out.

Change was not my friend.

Not only was everything new and different, but it seemed that my hopes and dreams were constantly diminishing. I wanted to reenlist, but I was denied. I wanted to start a business, but I was too depressed to get up and make anything happen. The only thing that remained constant and close to me was music. My depression led to drug dependency, which led to substance abuse (we'll talk more about this later), which only led to a deeper depression.

About a year later, someone made me an offer that I absolutely could not refuse. I was sitting in one of the meeting rooms at Battalion playing on a grand piano that was donated to the Wounded Warriors. I was releasing my bad day into a song when a sharply dressed man followed the noise and walked into the room. He introduced himself, and we struck up a conversation. He was from Syracuse University and was promoting a course for entrepreneurial veterans.

The Entrepreneurship Bootcamp for Veterans (EBV) is a month-long, intensive collegiate course that teaches veterans how to set up businesses and begin life as an entrepreneur after the military. After our conversation and after telling him about my journey and plans to start a nonprofit, teaching music therapy, he told me that I would be a perfect fit for the program and soon e-mailed me an application. I just wanted to get away for a couple weeks, and I thought that this would be a great little vacation. As it turns out, it was a pivotal turning point in my life.

I dove in headfirst. I put everything I had into studying and reading about entrepreneurialism. The more I read and learned about being an entrepreneur, the more I realized that this was my calling. I was nervous about leaving the Marine Corps, mainly because I felt like I had no skills that would transpose into the real world. I discovered the exact opposite: the Marine Corps gave me the most indispensable skills and methods for utilizing my talents. The Corps taught me to adapt and overcome. It taught me the art of situational awareness and time management. Being an entrepreneur means problem solving: adapting to a situation and developing a solution. At its root, the Marine Corps gave me the exact tools I needed to be an entrepreneur. I went to Syracuse University with an idea, and after graduation, I left with a well-structured plan, prepared to turn my dream into reality.

I came back to San Diego full of life, ready to take on the world. I was still scared about leaving the

Corps, but I was determined, now more than ever, to live. I went back to my daily grind at work, only now my days were spent polishing my business plan and implementing my music therapy program.

I started teaching music lessons at Wounded Warrior Battalion and got involved with a local recording studio. I saw some of the most incredible Marines crawl out of their darkest depression in our short musical sessions. I witnessed, firsthand, lives being changed though music. Watching these men and women take their combat experiences and turn them into beautiful songs gave me more reason to live than ever before.

Though I thought that I had found my purpose and had ignited a passion to dream once more, my insatiable appetite for my drugs and my unbridled self-hatred claimed those dreams. On the surface life seemed pretty good, but below the mask there was nothing but emptiness.

[The Monster in the Addict]

I merely existed as an *it*. I wasn't even human anymore. I was still a Marine, but I couldn't work like I used to, because I was considered a patient; and I was a patient that would not accept recovery. I was married, but I wasn't a husband. I could barely take care of myself. How was I supposed to take care of and support my wife? I was alive, sure, but I had no life in me. I became captive to my own demons— demons that surfaced from a deep, dreadful sea of self-pity and doubt. Those demons latched on to my darkest emotions like blood-hungry leeches and molested my weakened spirit. I turned into a monster of a man.

Saturday, February 1, 2014, is a day that I will remember for the rest of my life. I was hiking through the magnificent Giant Sequoia Grove in Yosemite National Park, and it hit me. I could see everything.

For the first time in years, my head was clear, and I could actually see every detail that was created to be seen—and it was breathtaking. There was no Percocet or methadone drowning out my senses. There was no whiskey numbing my emotions or clouding my vision. Everything in front of me was clear and colorful.

It is a truly amazing thing when you are able to see the world clearly and in color—exactly how it is meant to be seen.

For far too long, my world was colorless. For five years in the Marine Corps, I was trained to see the world in black and white: right and wrong, good and evil. There was no room for anything but a black-and-white mentality when you were preparing to go to war. It was either good, or it was evil. Anything but that left room for error, and the smallest error was the difference between life and death.

> *It is a truly amazing thing when you are able to see the world clearly and in color—exactly how it is meant to be seen.*

When I came home from war, black-and-white vision turned seamlessly to an all-encompassing black. My once simple and semi-innocent world view was now polluted with an indomitable hatred and a deep-seeded mistrust for all things living.

The copious amounts of drugs blurred not only days together but also months. I began making choices that drove my promising life into the ground. I went from having everything I could have ever imagined to being alone, eventually homeless, and sleeping in my car. It was my own fault, truthfully. I didn't *lose* anything; I threw it away in a fit of hopelessness.

I had a reconstructed spine. I had persistent joint pain. I had sore bones due to the chronic arthritis plaguing my sternum, hands, and back. Migraines were a daily occurrence. I had insomnia that kept me awake for days on end, and when I *did* sleep, my nightmares were violently out of control. I was diagnosed with post-traumatic stress disorder (PTSD), and the solution was, what else—drugs. "Give him so many drugs, because sick people need drugs."

Every morning I got out of bed and took my numbing concoction of methadone, Percocet, and oxycodone. I washed those delicious treats down with six additional pills, which of course, I *had to have* for various other ailments. Lunchtime no longer meant lunch; it meant time to take more pills. Every four hours I was popping a handful of Percocet, and whenever I felt like I needed to, I would choke down three or four methadones—just to take the edge off. Every two weeks, I pumped my bloodstream full of ketamine via medical infusion.

It wasn't long before I was an addict, though I would never have admitted it. I lived my fading life from pill to pill. Nothing mattered to me anymore. I found pleasure in nothing. The things that I used to enjoy no longer brought me any satisfaction. I used to be two hundred pounds of solid muscle, spending every spare minute of my busy days working out and focusing on my fitness: I swam and surfed the ocean daily; I played sports, and just for the fun of it, I went on marathon-length runs.

Now, I was high—all the time. I was a walking, breathing, and sometimes talking zombie. The most dangerous aspect of my type of high was that it was not only legal, but it was medically encouraged. Once a month my prescriptions were filled, and I went home unknowingly leashed to a very unforgiving master.

In the beginning of my recovery, I *needed* medications, but after a while, I just wanted them. I craved them. I knew all the right responses to give to my doctors when I went to my pain-management and medication-refill appointments. I knew exactly what I had to do to get more drugs.

After a few years of appointments and medication refills, the hospital began sending all of my prescriptions to my doorstep without even seeing if I still needed them.

I became accustomed to being on drugs. It became normal for me. I stopped noticing the life-altering effects and simply accepted my life as it was. I told myself I was a survivor, and these drugs were just a part of my survival now.

I began using my PTSD diagnosis as an excuse for my drug addiction. It was my ultimate crutch. My friends and family were noticing major changes in me, but I refused to acknowledge them. I became angry toward anyone who told me that I was acting differently.

My life was quickly spiraling out of control, and I blamed everything and everyone around me. All I could see was my own selfishly motivated desires, and the big picture was impossible to focus on. Truthfully, there was no big picture, because I felt as though I would be dead in a short matter of time anyway.

The worse my life got, the more I depended on my medications to solve my problems. I knew it wouldn't actually solve anything, but it *did* provide me a short escape from my problems.

I began doing things that were quite abnormal to the man I used to be. I was married, and I took vows to support and love my wife, but as soon as she started telling me that I was different and that I should probably dial back on my meds, my love for her turned to resentment. I blamed her for whatever I could. She was *supposed* to support me. She was *supposed* to be helping with me recovery.

Reality was that she *was* supporting me. She was trying to save my life.

She loved me deeply, but my drugs were telling me that she hated me. My drugs told me that I was incapable of being loved. My drugs told me that she was selfish. My drugs told me that she didn't—and couldn't ever—possibly understand what I was going through. I trusted my drugs, because they made me feel good. My drugs were deceitful, but I loved them, and I believed they were the only things that wanted to help me.

I cut off everyone who meant anything to me and isolated myself to my own depressing misery. I felt nothing. I was an emotionless monster. Not only was my pain numbed but so was my very existence—at least, so I thought. I wasn't emotionless at all. I was angry. I was bitter. I was resentful. I was hateful. Those emotions were all heightened as I delved deeper into my drug addiction.

It's a monstrous lie told to us by drugs: *Take me. I will make you numb. It will feel better.* We believe it: if we are numb, we will *feel* better. *I* believed it. Well,

I'm here to tell you that it doesn't help; it destroys. It nearly destroyed me. It brought out a beast inside of me. My anger—no, my rage—was unparalleled, and the second that succulent poison entered into my being, a grand transformation ensued. It was the ultimate reality of Dr. Jekyll and Mr. Hyde. I was a monster, in every sense of the word. I was dangerous and uncaged. I was unpredictable. My humanity was a distant memory. Even those closest to me, especially Aimee, didn't know who or what I was.

My wife—she not only endured the fiery wake of my destruction and demise, but she had the ungodly pleasure of watching it from the front row. She battled the monster face to face. This wasn't a fairy-tale fight where good heroically vanquished the evil foe and lived happily ever after with Prince Charming. This was a nightmare-from-hell kind of fight: the kind of fight where bloodshed and tears fill oceans, and pretty things are trampled on and killed. For you to truly understand, I am going to let *her* tell you the truth about me—about *it*. (She wrote this in 2013.)

My Husband Is a Drug Addict
by Aimee R. Fite

I have denied it for three years. I have sworn to anyone who will listen to me that he's "not actually addicted" and only takes the amount necessary to manage his pain—finding pride in that. For the first year, I became his pain manager. Fresh out of college, dreaming of starting a job with J. Crew at 770 Broadway in New York City, becoming a fashion mogul, I somehow found myself married and handing out pain pills to this monster of a man.

Some days, I hate him. Most nights, I'm consumed by the thought that I might wake up next to a corpse. He's always high. He has a valid excuse. But he's always high.

When we were getting engaged, my pain-management skills were one of the things he mentioned during our engagement: not my beauty, my intellect, my kind heart, or my sweet spirit—just how I carry around pills of oxycodone and methadone like a champion.

Shortly after we were married, I began our routine of managing his medications. Every six hours: two or three or four more pills, depending on the pain level. I wasn't a wife—just a drug dealer. I would watch the opiates surge through his veins twenty-three minutes after taking each dose of medication. His eyes would roll back; he'd slur a little; and depending on the cocktail of medications I had just served up, he would either become "the monster" or fall asleep.

I mostly prayed he'd fall asleep, deeply fearing the other outcome.

Under the influence, he was raw and unpredictable. He'd flash back vividly to moments of time in Afghanistan, thrash in his sleep, and lash out at me in wild outbursts of anger or rage. I found myself loving and hating the drugs all at the same time but also trying desperately to separate the man from the monster in my mind so that I could keep attempting to love my husband through this.

One particular night, when we lived in our small loft apartment in Carlsbad, I learned firsthand just how powerful the monster really was. We had just had a fight about something insignificant, and shortly after that he took his medication. We decided to head to bed, hoping that sleep would calm the storm and allow us to think more clearly in the morning. After I thought that he was asleep, I began to quietly sob. My feelings were hurt; I felt unloved; and I needed to let it out. Not even five minutes of quiet tears had passed when he suddenly turned me over onto my back and shook me violently by the shoulders.

"Stop crying! *Stop crying*! JUST STOP CRYING!" I had never been touched by a man in this manner, and more importantly, I refused to be touched in this way by my husband. Startled and scared, I began to sob wildly. I got up out of our bed, and he began to chase me through the house. I grabbed the keys to the car, ran down the steps, and got in. He came stalking out at me and began to punch and bang on the windows of the car, yelling at me: "Get in the house!"

I was terrified.

His eyes were black and filled with rage: the pupils were so dilated that no color could be seen. He was screaming obscenities at me while pounding on the hood of the car, and I felt paralyzed with fear. I finally pressed one shaking foot down on the gas pedal and drove to the only safe place I could think of at the time—our church. I sat in the parking lot of that church and prayed and cried out to God for about an hour.

I returned home to find my husband gone. He had driven his motorcycle up to the barracks and had sent me a very short text message telling me that he'd be sleeping there.

We never talked about that incident again. He never acknowledged what happened, and when I tried to bring it up, he shut me down. I will never forget the terror or the absolute horror of staring into the face of the man I loved, knowing that he had just forever turned himself into a monster in my mind.

I believed he stopped taking the pills in September 2012. At least, that's what he told everyone: that he was clean and tired of the way the pills made him feel. Hell, he even posted on Facebook about it!

Once he was off the drugs, things proceeded to go downhill for us. He would disappear at nights, rarely answering his cell phone or texts. He became wild, unruly, undisciplined, and hateful—*hateful* really was the best word to describe him. He hated me and had no qualms about showing it.

No matter how much I loved him, fought for him, fought with him, advocated for him—no matter what I did—it was never enough. He would spew venom at me as if the anger, rage, and hurt he was dealing with were somehow my fault.

But I'm writing this in April 2013, and I am staring at the face of the monster I know all too well, and today, I know that this is the beginning of the end. I know it's been this way for a while for us—but truly, the end is here.

I came home from an exhausting day of work and found him, as usual, sprawled out on our couch, staring into the television screen. He never actually watches it. I think he wants me to think he's involved in the show so that we won't have to have conversation. The house was a disaster. Not one of the small requests I made had been dealt with today. These small things just added to my exhaustion, and I instantly felt as if I would collapse.

I sat down, wanting nothing more than to be held by this man next to me—to be cherished, adored, and have him turn his face toward me as I spoke; to have him run his fingers through my hair and down my spine in a gentle, comfortable way; to have his arm wrapped around the small of my back and feel his fingers lightly caress my skin. I wanted these things so badly, I ached for them.

Nothing in the world will break a woman to pieces like love withheld, and I cannot remember a time when I felt love in our home. My spirit is broken, and my heart is empty. I want his attention—even the semblance of attention would do at this point—but I sit here, quietly, and I start to sob: for my exhaustion, for the dirty dishes, for the time three years ago when I first learned to fear the monster, for all the words I've never said, for all my worry and fear, for the unmet needs, and for love. I always cry over love.

He doesn't look up or over. And I start to talk. I've gotten used to talking to this wall of a man. As ugly as it sounds, I've become very good at being ignored.

"Today was so emotionally exhausting. I'm so tired, Brad. I'm just so tired. I need help. Are you listening? Do you hear me? I need you. I don't know if I can do all of this anymore. I don't even know if I can do 'this' anymore. I need your help. I need *you*."

Somehow, this sobbing and confession of exhaustion stir him. He sits up and looks at me, stone-faced. He proceeds to confess that since September he has been abusing his medications—sometimes taking upward of six at a time, three to six times a day, and that's just what I knew of.

The words he spoke all ran together, and I picked up bits and pieces of things like "drugs" and "need them" and "want to be high." The most striking part was the "I like to be numb." I tuned into that statement so well and decided that was how I would feel: numb.

I shut myself off today. I felt my emotions leave. I have never felt more lied to in my life. After all I have endured with this man, I certainly don't deserve...this. I want to run away. I want to hide. I decided today that I would never, ever let him love me—no matter what.

I'm going to die today.

My time in the Marines was coming to a close, and I was now pursuing a career in the music industry. In what seemed to be the blink of an eye, red carpets, celebs, courtside seats, money, and drugs were all I cared about. I told myself that this was what I wanted and convinced myself that nothing else—and I do mean *nothing*—mattered.

I didn't have a lot of money, and I couldn't afford the finer things in life that everyone else around me had, so I began selling drugs to make up for the funds that I was lacking. I had the picture-perfect future right in front of me, but I was too ignorant to see beyond the pain of my present brought about by the misfortune of my past. I had the audacity to divorce my amazing wife and in turn took my drug addiction to the next level.

The misery in me had finally found its company. I cannot adequately express to you the immensity of my sins. I was so much more than a hateful drug addict; I was, in every sense of the word, a monster. *Honor*, *courage,* and *commitment* were three words that I had not only lived by but had also nearly died by. The words *shameful* and *cowardly* now summarized my character well. I was a disgrace of a human, and it pains me to admit that to you.

My drug dealing led me into some very dark places—but none as dreadful as the one I am now going to share with you.

***

I had been selling for about three months, and due to the class of network I was now affiliated with, I was brought to a place where I was told I could take my "business" to the next level—dog fights: cowards, betting on and reaping pleasure from beautiful animals ripping each other from limb to limb, all in the name of entertainment. I hated it, truly and passionately. I cringed every time I entered a dog coliseum; but money was good, and I craved money almost as much as I craved my drugs. I never bet on or even watched an actual fight, I just sold my drugs and took my leave when I was emptied out.

One night I was urged to stay all the way to the completion of the night's events, which again was not something I had really ever done. I stayed, and at the end of the night, four men took center stage and fought each other like they themselves were animals. I couldn't watch the dogs fight, but for some reason, I was instinctively drawn to the human fights. It was brutal, and I was hooked.

Instantly I wanted in and asked what I had to do to fight. I was told that I just had to pay a fee. I didn't have a lot of money, but I did have thousands of narcotics. I offered him a trade: my drugs for his fights. He agreed, and just like that I was on the card.

My first fight was against a middle-aged man standing nearly a foot taller than I was and outweighing me by at least sixty pounds. I looked like anything but a fighter. I looked like a haggard drug addict that needed to fight for his next fix. I was about 145 pounds of pale skin and sunken bones with a soul as black as the night. When I stepped into the "ring," which was really only ten by ten-*ish* square feet roped off by duct tape around four blocks of concrete, I felt a rush of calmed rage come over me. It felt good. The crowd gathered around, and in excitement they clapped their hands and placed their blood-money bets.

The fight was on.

He pranced over to me, eyes fixed on my face, left arm outstretched and right arm cocked back by his ear.

Let me guess, he's coming for my face with that right hand.

I didn't even have to duck to avoid it. As his arm went flying over me, my hands clinched to the back of his neck, and my perfectly placed right knee powered into his beer-filled abdomen; he puked on contact. The pack of wolves watching the action from behind the tape screamed with approval. I felt empowered as they roared. I looked down, and the man was on his knees with both arms stretched out onto the floor. I felt a rush of validation and acceptance as my shin crashed into his face in perfect sync to the howls of the bystanders. I felt free.

I felt—I *felt* something else besides depression and hate. It was the release and rush that I had been searching for. For the first time in years I felt good. I wanted to hold on to this feeling forever, but within minutes of the fight ending, it dissipated, and again I was left in just as much despair as ever. I had to feel this again. I now craved it nearly as much as I craved my drugs. I continued fighting in secret for months. If only for a few minutes, my rage, remorse, regret, and hate had somewhere to go.

With each fight I took, the adrenaline rush and emotional release of the fight would wear off little by little. It started getting to the point where I felt just as numb fighting as I did *not* fighting, so I started taking fights that I couldn't win: sometimes taking fights against three or four guys at a time. I wasn't searching for an adrenaline rush anymore, nor was I searching to release my emotions; it was a reckless search for atonement. I told myself, still, that my friend was dead because of me; therefore, I deserved to feel pain.

I would get absolutely wrecked in these fights. I'd wake up in a puddle of my own blood, wherever they decided to leave my body. I again told myself that I deserved this. The pain of realizing that I was a train wreck and had crashed my life drove me deeper and deeper and deeper into this lifestyle. It felt good to be beaten and bloodied. It felt good to be given what I thought my behavior merited. It was nothing more than a sick form of penance for what I assured myself were my crimes. I became more and more reckless with my life and finally concluded that my life was no longer worth living. My rage effortlessly turned to hopelessness, and my hate was turned inward. I hated more than anything this monster I became.

I devised a plan to die and wanted to end it all exactly where I thought I belonged. It wasn't long until the perfect death came to my ear. I was offered an opportunity to attend a party at which I would be expected to sell drugs as well as fight. It was cheap. It was dirty. It was dangerous. It was *perfect*.

The fights that night were to take place in an emptied-out in-ground pool, in the backyard of a run-down gangland house in East Los Angeles. I pulled up to a house that appeared to have some fire damage and drove a block down the street, where I parked. I opened up a bottle of eighteen-year-old Glenfiddich malt Scotch whiskey that I had been saving for some time. I didn't know exactly what I was saving it for, but I knew it was going to be a hell of an event when I finally decided to break its seal.

I sat in my car, alone and unafraid, with music blaring from my speakers as I washed down a suicidal concoction of methadone and oxycodone with my beloved whiskey. I would look right and then quickly look to my left, and judging by how long it took my vision to catch up, I could gage my readiness for the night's event. I didn't want to be *too* drunk though, so I burned my arm with my cigarettes to make sure I could still feel the pain. I *needed* to feel every ounce of pain. I finished wiping down my .45 caliber Springfield for probably the twentieth time and slid it back under my driver's seat. If the fight didn't kill me tonight, this would have to do the trick.

I passed out in the driver's seat of my car and was suddenly awakened by three men standing outside my door. They hit my window and told me that I should get off their street and go back to where I belonged. If they only knew. I snatched my keys out of the ignition and opened my door; the three men all jumped backward and waved the pungent odor of alcohol and smoke away from their faces.

"You tryin' to get yourself killed, white boy?"

I didn't say a word. I just closed the door and walked up the block, heading to the address where I planned to die that night. I walked straight through the crowded party and into the backyard. I was snatched up by the regulator of the night, and to say that he was not happy with me is a massive understatement. Due to passing out in my car, I had inadvertently missed my fight. He grabbed me at the neck and slammed me up against the deteriorating brick wall of the house.

My first thought was to just fight *him*, kill him, incite a riot at the house, and get killed by the men loyal to him. He told me that he was glad I was dumb enough to still show up even after my fight had passed, because now he had something even better planned for me. He walked me over to the emptied-out pool, where four dogs were locked in cages at the bottom. The floor of the pool was covered in broken glass bottles, cigarette butts, and trash from the evening. Two of the dogs were taken out from their cages and replaced with my new opponent and me.

I now sat in the bottom of a dirty, disgusting pool—caged; the partygoers stood above me, looking down, laughing, and eventually urinating on me. More and more glass bottles were being thrown down into the pool at the cages, shattering and sending glass shrapnel into the cage and into my flesh.

I wasn't enraged. I wasn't even mad. I was at complete peace.

This—this was *exactly* where I belonged. This was *exactly* how I deserved to die.

This was officially rock bottom.

The plan was to give the party an epic showcase to finish off the night by having my opponent and me fight at the same time the dogs would fight—one epic bloody and disgusting battle.

I was slowly drifting into black again, and so I curled up in the cage and closed my eyes while I waited for my moment to take center stage—one final time.

I opened my eyes a while later to find that a smoky fog covered all that my dilated eyes could see, but it appeared that confusion was erupting above as blinding lights began lasering across the dark yard above me. A light, seeming like something brighter than I had ever experienced before, shone directly on me, literally blinding me.

A sharp pain began thrashing inside my head, and I quickly turned over to escape the painful light. A man rushed down the steep walls of the pool and knelt beside my cage. He began asking me questions, trying to figure out if I was a threat or if I could be let out. He unlocked my cage and helped me out of the pool. He asked me who I was and what the chances were that I had any identification on me. I told him in mumbles that I had left all my identification in my car. He noticed my Marine Corps tattoos and asked me if I was a Marine.

He asked again, and I finally replied with a yeah.

He grabbed my arm and said, "Let's go."

He sat me on a curb behind the house, away from the commotion, and told me not to move. I didn't have the energy to move.

Moments later he whipped around the corner and pulled his unmarked police car up to the curb. He got out and helped me into the front passenger seat and began prepping my arm for an IV. After the needle was jammed into my arm, he gave me the fluid bag, and while shaking his head in disappointment, he said, "Hold this."

I lodged the bag in between my hand and my head, and reality began to sink in. He didn't say anything for a while, which I wasn't complaining about, but finally, he spoke.

"You're gonna kill yourself, kid"—a phrase, more like a mantra by now, that I had been hearing in my head for months. Little did he know that was exactly the plan.

Over the course of two IV bags he told me about his own experiences in the Marine Corps, specifically of his tours in Iraq, and in grave detail, he told me about his own life after death. He assured me that life after war would never be easy, but that I had the power to make it better, and I was in control of that. He repeated: *"Not easy…but better."*

I'm [not] going to die today.

I had to make a change. My life was in shambles, and I knew I was on the fast track to death. I felt like I was on a runaway train, heading for a brick wall, and I couldn't stop it, nor could I get off.

I woke up a few mornings later, reached over to the wobbly, stained nightstand by my bed, and instinctively grabbed a handful of my pills. I took a swig of the warm, two- or three-day-old beer and swallowed my day's first dose of "medication." I rolled onto my back, my head pounding. I closed my eyes, and the officer's voice came thundering back into my head: "You're gonna kill yourself, kid."

I jumped out of bed, ran into my bathroom, and shoved my grimy fingers down my throat, forcing myself to throw up the meds that were just beginning to take action in my veins. I stood up, and my feeble frame staggered over the sink. The iron-saturated tap water began washing out my post-puke mouth. I thought it again. Only this time, for some reason I didn't just think it, I said it out loud: "*BRAD! STOP! You're gonna die.*"

It was almost like the thing in the mirror was talking to me. It was a strange feeling: for the first time in a long time, something inside of me did *not* want to die. I knew what I had to do, but what I *couldn't* do was another hospital or any form of treatment.

I had a paralyzing fear of hospitals at this point, and even the thought of being back inside of one caused intense panic attacks. I knew that if I went into a program, there would be some form of therapist or, even worse, more psych docs. I couldn't handle any more of those either. By this time, I had been through fourteen therapists/counselors/doctors.

I had to do this on my own. Was that the smartest plan of attack? Not a chance, but I knew I could do it, and I knew I *had* to do it.

I tried mentally preparing myself for the next however many days; but in actuality I wasn't preparing myself. I was doing everything I could to convince myself *not* to do what I was about to do. My stomach was cramping, and I was feigning for my fix.

I had no idea what was about to happen. The longest I had made it without a drug in my failing system was a mere few hours, and within those first few hours, my body would begin to rage against me, until I fed it what it required. I stood in the bathroom, and as I beheld my reflection in the mirror, I wrote "LIVE" in huge letters across the glass. I then took all the pills I had and poured them into the toilet. Over ten thousand tabs of narcotic painkillers—flushed away. And so it began.

BRAD C. FITE

The first day without my drugs wasn't really *that* bad. It wasn't, by any means, a walk in the park either. But compared to what I thought might happen, it wasn't that bad.

That first night, though, it began to hit me. I tried sleeping, but my anxiety was through the roof. I couldn't seem to stop sweating, and my stomach was turning in knots. My hands and fingers were aching, and my legs were more restless than ever. I tried watching TV, but my head was pounding, and the light from the screen was making me nauseous.

Over the next week, my mind and body deteriorated into what I thought, and what felt like, was the worst of it. I spent days on end curled up on a tiled bathroom floor, waiting for the next certain puking episode. I had nothing left in my stomach, but somehow, distinctly pungent bile kept expelling itself from inside of me. I was miserable but held on to the fact that tomorrow had to come at some point...and then the next day...and the next. At some point, this misery had to end. At least, that's what I kept telling myself.

Day twelve of my withdrawal process was particularly memorable to me. I awoke from my half kind of sleep with an intolerable desire for my drugs. *I had to have them!* I spent the majority of the day curled up on my bed, sweating profusely but somehow freezing cold, and for some reason that I could not understand, I had a burning aching throughout my hands and fingers.

My nausea once again got the better of me, and I stumbled into the bathroom. I heaved and heaved, but nothing would come out. It only intensified my stomach and abdominal cramps.

I stared into the toilet basin and remembered all the drugs I had flushed into it several days ago. I knew that there *had* to be some remnants of those drugs left in the water. I scooped the poisoned toilet water into my mouth and convinced myself that it was making me high. Within minutes I had something to puke up, and I did; I hurled every last drop. I passed out again on the floor. I woke up with the most incredible and agonizing pain in my chest, and as I was gasping for air, I remember thinking, "This is it...I'm dying."

I grew up in a house of faith and surrounded by people of prayer. I went to church three days a week and even went to a Christian school. I quit believing in my parents' God while I was in Afghanistan. I didn't want anything to do with a God that would so unjustly allow this kind of pain in His world and within His creation that He so deeply loved. I created my own personal image of "god," and to me he was nothing more than a coward and a liar. Where was he when I needed him the most? Where was he now?

I prayed for the first time in years, and in a moment of absolute surrender, I begged God to give me breath. In that moment, I heard a voice tell me to breathe. I thought someone had come into my room and was standing directly above me—but no one was there. I felt a rush of peace come over me, and in an instant my chest pain dissipated into nothing. I breathed freely, and I knew that I was *not* going to die that day.

I took the experiences and the pain of that day, and I wrote a song called B*reathe.*

The pain I feel I try to forget.
The armor I wear is remorse and regret.
I'm drowning now; I must get air.
Breathe, my child; do not despair.
You're drowning now,
But soon you'll be free.
Call on my name,
And in me you will breathe.

So
Breathe in me;
Breathe in me.

My heart is open to the lies of this place.
Seeing the glory but forgetting the grace.
My brothers looked back, and they turned to stone.
My sisters awoke, afraid and alone.
I'm running now, my foot soon to bleed—
Desperate for life, desperate to breathe.

So
Breathe in me;
Breathe,
Breathe in me.
I'm begging for love.
You beg me to seek.
I'm clinging to life;
I barely can breathe.
So breathe, breathe in me.

After seventeen days of enduring the most viscous

physical pain I've ever experienced due to

withdrawing from my drugs, I walked out of my room

and swore to myself and to my God that I would never again touch drugs. The monster was defeated, but it was not dead, nor do I believe that it will ever be gone forever. It is and will continue to be a battle that I must personally—and daily—choose to fight.

I came so close to dying, and I watched firsthand as friends of mine died. I lived like the popular saying, "Live like you're dying." I made a decision to change that. I don't want to live my life like I'm going to die tonight; I want to live like I'm going to be alive tomorrow.

IMPROVISE, ADAPT & OVERCOME

The terms *improvise*, *adapt*, and *overcome* were engrained into my hard head in the early stages of boot camp, as an eager young recruit. These three simple words have become the unofficial mantra of the United States Marine Corps, and they couldn't be more fitting.

This slogan originally referred to the weapons and substandard equipment the Marines were given to fight with, mostly consisting of hand-me-downs from the Army. The Marines had no other choice but to improvise, adapt, and overcome with what they were given. They had to find a way to use whatever resources were available to win their wars. This mantra has proven to take on a much more personal meaning to me throughout the years. It is a lifestyle. It's a manner in which I *choose* to live my life—no matter what—day in and day out. At its root, it means: find a way to *survive*, and then *thrive*.

It doesn't just stop at surviving. It urges us to conquer whatever lies before us. Life is going to continuously throw us curveballs that seem to put a dent in our plans at every twist in our wild adventure of a story, and with every curveball, we need to have tools ready to combat them.

Phase I – Improvise

im·pro·vise

ˈimprəˌvīz

verb

Produce or make (something) from whatever is available

More than once in my twenty-six years of life, I have had to implement improvisation techniques, but never more so than I did after my injury.

After awakening from my coma, I was told that I would (most likely) never walk again. The damage to my spine was just too severe. I spent many months trying to come to grips with life in a wheelchair and reacted, understandably, with a less-than-stellar attitude toward my unfortunate situation. Little by little I began improvising, and little by little, I began making small improvements in my life.

Improvise does not mean to do whatever it takes to *change* your situation. Too many times I tried controlling my surroundings—to no avail. I was just frantically surviving: trying to control and change every little thing that came my way, and nothing good comes out of frantic reactions.

> I spent all of my time denying my past, which ultimately rendered me incapable of focusing on building a wonderful future.

I realized that there was not much in life that I could actually control; whatever was going to happen was going to happen. However, I could choose to make the best out of my current situation, as hard as that might seem.

Improvising means that you are using what is available. I was having the hardest time trying to improvise, because I was consistently rejecting my present circumstance. I spent all of my time denying my past, which ultimately rendered me incapable of focusing on building a wonderful future.

While in the improvise phase of my recovery, I discovered two of my greatest enemies: passivity and fear.

It was the passivity of waiting on time to heal me that was slowly destroying me. In order to properly improvise, I had to reject this spirit of passivity and become a man of constant and adamant forward movement. I could not allow myself to be comfortable waiting on anything or anyone to do something for me—especially when it came to my personal healing.

Multiple times I was told, "Brad, time heals all wounds; just give it time."

Seriously? Time doesn't actually heal anything, and that's just the brutal truth. If you are relying on time to heal your wound, good luck. If you've been shot and you have a bullet hole in you, you can't just sit back and say, "Oh, it's okay; I'll just let time heal it."

Sure, that wound may close, but it is going to get infected, and sooner or later, it's going to open back up uglier and more painful than ever. It can even become deadly. If you aren't actively healing and aren't caring for your wound, there's no chance of it getting better.

I would go in once a month to my pain-management appointments and beg my doctors to take me off my narcotics, but over and over again they told me, "You need time; you're still healing. Your body needs this. Just give it some more time."

I didn't fight it, because I had no fight left in me. I was so okay with just sitting back, getting high, and telling myself that tomorrow might be better. It was easier that way.

Constantly moving forward one tiny inch at a time with whatever tools are readily available is *improvising*.

There is a quotation that I would like to share with you from one of my favorite movies, *Any Given Sunday*. In the scene, Al Pacino's character, Tony D'Amato, is attempting to bring his self-destructing football team back together in the heat of battle:

I don't know what to say, really. Three minutes to the biggest battle of our professional lives. All comes down to today, and either, we heal as a team, or we're gonna crumble. Inch by inch, play by play. Until we're finished. We're in hell right now, gentlemen. Believe me. And, we can stay here, get the shit kicked out of us, or we can fight our way back into the light. We can climb outa hell...one inch at a time. Now I can't do it for ya, I'm too old. I look around, I see these young faces and I think, I mean, I've made every wrong choice a middle-aged man can make. I uh, I've pissed away all my money, believe it or not. I chased off anyone who's ever loved me. And lately, I can't even stand the face I see in the mirror.

You know, when you get old, in life, things get taken from you. I mean, that's...that's...that's a part of life. But, you only learn that when you start losin' stuff. You find out life's this game of inches, so is football. Because in either game— life or football—the margin for error is so small. I mean, one half a step too late or too early and you don't quite make it. One half second too slow, too fast and you don't quite catch it. The inches we need are everywhere around us. There is every break of the game, every minute, every second. On this team we fight for that inch. On this team we tear ourselves and everyone else around us to pieces for that inch. We claw with our fingernails for that inch. Because we know when we add up all those inches, that's gonna make the fucking difference between winning and losing! Between living and dying! I'll tell you this, in any fight it's the guy whose willing to die whose gonna win that inch. And I know, if I'm gonna have any life anymore it's because I'm still willing to fight and die for that inch, because that's what living is, the six inches in front of your face.

—Taken from *Any Given Sunday*
Screenplay by John Logan
Source: www.imdb.com

I had potential. I had a future. I had a promising life right in front of my face, and I was so focused on how much I was hurting that I nearly threw it all away, because I was overcome with a spirit of fear. I was paralyzed by the fear of failure. I had convinced myself that I was nothing more than a failure and would amount to nothing more than a pile of those failures; but how could I fail if I didn't do anything? Passivity and fear will crumble you; they crumbled me.

After I got clean off my drugs, I began living my life taking by pure force those inches one tiny decision at a time—one good decision followed by another. Easy thing to do? No, not at all. It's an extremely difficult thing to do; but it's worth it.

I began rejecting passivity and started living my life in constant forward movement, capturing every inch, and slowly but surely *life* started happening in me again.

I could have remained comfortably miserable, but that would have just killed me off. I put together a plan and adamantly chased the desired results. Months began flying by, and I started looking back on my life as it was and couldn't imagine what it would've been like had I stayed there dwelling in my complacency.

Opportunities once again came knocking on my door, and this time I was ready and willing to grab them and hold on to them; and I did much more than just that. I started dreaming again, and inch by painful inch I started making those dreams reality.

The first order of business was to get my wife back. That was a really painful grip of inches, but some things in life are truly worth fighting for, and Aimee was number one on the list of those things. My wife stuck by me and fought for me through everything, including a divorce. I had broken her precious heart time and time again, and so much of me told me that I didn't even *deserve* to have another chance with her. I was so afraid that if we *did* get back together I would just ruin it again and break the heart that I vowed to protect. The more I wanted her back, the more fear whispered lies into my head:

How could she possibly love me again?

How could she ever trust me again?

She deserves so much better than me.

It was time to start fighting for her. I *had* to fight for her—for us. We got back together, and in November 2014, we had our first son.

I also brought my foundation back to life and began teaching music therapy to other combat-wounded veterans from all over San Diego.

I began writing a book—obviously. (Thanks for buying it, by the way!)

I had compiled an album's worth of songs throughout the darkness that were the four and a half previous years of my life, and I was ready to bring them to life. Multiple times the fear that once crippled me resurfaced and attempted to pull me back into its enticing misery, but I kept clawing for those inches.

I remained on a forward track, fighting for my life and fighting for my dreams. Those dreams became a reality, and after forming my band, *The Makers,* the songs that storied my pain through music came to life in an album we titled *WAR Stories.*

After you claw your way through life's inches on your hands and knees, you stand; you pick yourself up, wipe away the dirt, and continue pressing forward directly into and unwaveringly through the next phase.

Phase II – Adapt

a·dapt

əˈdapt

verb

Make (something) suitable for a new use or purpose; modify.

Become adjusted to new conditions.

There is a key word in that definition that I, and most of us, seem to miss: *modify*. Adapting isn't just accepting surrounding situations and merely blending in. It means modifying your position to make your current circumstance better.

I wore my mask and tried blending in with the society surrounding me. I concealed everything about me in hopes that the world would just accept me or, worse, modify to *me*. What I failed to realize was that the struggles and hardships that we face make us who we are. Blending in isn't taking advantage; it's just...well...blending in. Adapting and bettering our lives leads to overcoming whatever situation we are in.

I found myself adapting in all the wrong ways, mainly because I had an overwhelming sense of entitlement. I felt like the world should have been adapting to *me*. Daily I thought, "I got blown up by a bomb; I shouldn't have to do anything anymore!" It was when I was diagnosed with PTSD that I encountered my first adaptation failure: medication. Well, the doctors said I had a disorder, so how else was I supposed to adapt? I adapted to my diagnosis normally: I flooded my mind and body with narcotic painkillers.

Let me interject briefly and say that taking medications is *not* wrong. I am *not* a doctor nor am I in any way certified to tell you whether or not you should be taking medications. But what I can tell you is what I did—and how I failed—in hopes that you will learn from me and, in turn, better your own life.

In 2010, as I said earlier, I was diagnosed with PTSD, and with that singular diagnosis, without proper education and research on the topic, my world spiraled downward. It allowed me the opportunity for a crutch. It allowed me to shift the responsibility of the ownership of my actions.

I would say, "I don't have an anger issue; I

> *I am not a victim unless I make the choice to claim that title.*

have ptsD." "I'm not isolating myself; I have ptsD." "I'm not depressed; I'm suffering from an incurable disorder called ptsD." I could go on for pages, but you get the idea.

I made myself the victim, and I fell into the role seamlessly. I am not a victim unless I make the choice to claim that title.

I have had the honor and privilege of serving under the grit and guidance of numerous leaders during my time in the Marines. One Marine Corps leader that I have always admired is General James Mattis, and I'd like you to read a quotation of his that I feel sums up everything I am trying to get across right now:

I would just say there is one misconception of our veterans and that is that they are somehow damaged goods. I don't buy it. If we tell our veterans enough that this is what is wrong with them they may actually start believing it. While victimhood in America is exalted I don't think our veterans should join those ranks. There is also something called post-traumatic growth where you come out of a situation like that and you actually feel kinder toward your fellow man and fellow woman. There is no room for military people, including our veterans, to see themselves as victims even if so many of our countrymen are prone to relish that role.

—General James Mattis
Source: www.USAToday.com

I experienced multiple exceedingly traumatic events. As those events unfolded, my brain, conscious or not, stored those events in a part of my brain called the limbic system. It was fail-safe. Once they were stored, my body was then naturally prepared to respond in a way in which its primary instinct was to protect me from anything that could trigger those memories from activating. Any physiological effects surrounding my traumatic event were stored as default. If any of those senses were activated— whether it was sight, smell, feel, touch, or taste—my body naturally reverted back to certain fail-safe settings. PTSD is nothing more than my body or mind responding normally to an abnormal situation.

So if it's normal, how can it be a disorder? I'm not saying PTSD is not real; don't interpret that in the wrong way. It's very, *very* real. What I *am* saying is that I personally do not believe that it is a disorder. I consider post-traumatic stress an instinctual protection mechanism that is in no way abnormal.

Seeing death is not normal. War is not normal. Sexual assault is not normal. Abuse is not normal; yet, the primary method of treatment for all of the above is medication to cope, not treatment to heal. And that, my friends, is where we engage adaptation.

If you recall back to my opening words in this letter to you, I said that movement is key to survival; well, adapting is movement, and it is key to survival. Adapting to geographical surroundings and to the customs of the local people are key factors in going to war, and adapting techniques translate directly into living life in full color afterward.

For me, it was something as simple as sports. I love sports, especially basketball, though soccer is a close second. I pursued soccer in college and excelled greatly in the sport, but my favorite was always basketball. My dad was a high school basketball coach, and I grew up watching him coach and hanging out at his practices with the team.

When I was in kindergarten, my parents put a basketball hoop up in my bedroom, which naturally led to countless hours of basketball battles between my older brother and me. I couldn't dunk on the rim, but I could jump off my dresser and make some pretty radical jams. Every summer I was in basketball camps, and that led to coaching camps as I grew older.

After I was injured in Afghanistan, I thought all hopes of playing the sport again were over. For a long time I allowed that thought to control me, and I just figured that it was what it was. Well, in 2012 I was approached to try out for the Marine Corps Wounded

Warrior wheelchair basketball team. I entered the Warrior Games Trials that year, and I not only played wheelchair basketball but swam and played seated volleyball. I don't know if you've ever seen wheelchair basketball or seated volleyball, but both are quite extreme. Most wheelchair basketball games turned into wheelchair rugby matches. So of course, I fell in love with it instantly! The rules are a bit different, obviously, and the style of play is different, but the goal of the game is still the same: get the ball through the hoop. I could play sports; I just had to adapt to what I thought were my setbacks.

It was there, at the 2012 Warrior Games, that I met the man who would become one of my best friends and greatest brothers, Paul De Gelder. Paul had been a very specialized operator in the Australian military. He was a clearance diver and was considered the elite of the elite. He was conducting counterterrorism training operations in the Sydney Harbor when a bull shark attacked him. The shark got away with Paul's right leg and hand, but Paul got away with the help of his team saving his life. Now one would think that loosing your arm and leg would be a major setback, but despite his obvious limitations, Paul became limitless in his lifestyle and in his pursuit of living, proving that adaptation is not only possible, but it's worth the work. He now travels the world, speaking and sharing his story of survival and hope. You can even find him on Discovery Channel's *Shark Week*. He is a real-life hero of mine, and if it weren't for him, his friendship, and his inspiration, I would not be here writing this to you.

Earlier, in 2011, I met another man that proved to me that living after death was not only possible but within my reach.

My neighbor George was a ninety-six-year-young Marine Corps veteran. He had lived through one of the harshest battles ever fought and had seen terrors of war that my mind could not even fathom. After surviving a tour of duty in the Pacific, George was handpicked by Lieutenant General Lewis Burwell "Chesty" Puller to lead a platoon of Marines directly into and through North Korea's merciless Chosin Reservoir. George and his Marines, known now as *The Chosin*, fought a seventeen-day battle in the harshest of conditions that would be forever revered in history books as one of the most legendary victories in the Marine Corps.

George made his way down to the apartment complex's pool every morning as the sun rose and pushed himself through an aquatic workout. I would also spend a lot of time at the pool, because water workouts were about all that I could handle. George would always be in the corner of the pool, circling his arms under the water with small foam water weights. I always just thought he was elderly and doing an "old-person workout." I could not have been more wrong. One morning, after watching me hobble my way into the pool, George struck up a conversation with me.

"Where'd you snag up them zippers?" (referring to my scars) he asked me.

I told him that I was in the Marine Corps, and he grinned, winked an eye, and rumbled out, "Ooh-rah," which was subsequently followed by a low string of laughs.

I started telling him about my deployment into Afghanistan and the injuries I sustained from the bomb. I filled him in on my recovery and my current situation. After I was done rambling, I asked George about his service, and with one question to this man, my life would be forever impacted.

"So what about you, George? What'd you do?"

He chuckled and said, "I froze my ass off."

I laughed, confused, and just said, "Yeah?"

"The dammed best, worst days of my damn life," he said reminiscently.

"So...uh...what'd you get to do?" I asked him.

"I won wars and bled with the best." He smiled, and then he leaned in and said, "Tell me, young gun, what'd they teach you about the Chosin Reservoir?" Then he winked and went back to his workout.

"You fought in the Chosin Reservoir?"

"Yeah," he responded with a deep sigh.

He cleared his throat and said, "And I've been fighting that fight ever since."

Over the span of the next five months, George and I would sit down by the pool, almost daily, and he would tell me all about his time in the Corps and his fearless time in war.

He told me, in grave detail, the horrors of the Chosin battle. He valiantly fought with his beloved Corps, extremely outnumbered, for days on end in subzero temperatures against the relentless enemy. He hid under piles of dead warriors to escape the wrathful bullets of the enemy and the freezing nights. It was so cold that their eyes would freeze open, and any open skin would be subject to frostbite. He took me day by day through one of the most storied fights in the history of the Marine Corps. I was amazed and shocked to hear George's stories. Every time he spoke, my mind was absolutely blown away. I couldn't even imagine the terrors he had experienced.

George was unable to walk on his own—thus, his aquatic workouts. After a three-day fight and a twenty-mile march into a new zone, George had sat down to be examined by a corpsman. He had taken off his boot, and with his boot had come the bottom of his foot.

"Hold on, George. So what did you do when your foot came off?"

"Well, I strapped my damn boot back on! How else was I supposed to keep my foot on? It wasn't really too tough, until my fingers started coming off. Then I was in a damn pickle."

Blown away by this man's grit, I asked him how he did it all—how he made it through everything.

His answer was simple: "The same way you're making it through. We adapt, and then we overcome. We're Devil Dogs, ain't we?"

After the Marine Corps, George got married to a beautiful bride and raised four sons with her. He supported his family as an electrical engineer and worked the next thirty years as a simple man, enjoying the simple pleasures of life. As he told me about his life after combat, I was filled with hope.

He is a constant and shining example to me of the possibilities of life. If he can have a life after the things he experienced, I have no excuse not to live.

> *I have to make the daily choice to adapt to whatever situation may come.*

The will to adapt to a new kind of normal is a daily choice; and it is a choice that is not easy.

The way I swore to fight for my country and the way in which George—and so many others—fought for freedom is the same kind of tenacity with which I choose to fight for my life today. I must choose to engage my indomitable spirit and fight for my life. I have to make the daily choice to adapt to whatever situation may come.

Phase III – Overcome

o·ver·come

ōvərˈkəm

verb

Defeat (an opponent); prevail.

In 1519, a Spanish conquistador by the name of Hernando Cortez devised a plan to conquer the Aztec Empire and claim all of its storied treasures for his beloved country. Cortez brought his quest before the king and queen and was granted eleven ships, five hundred soldiers, and one hundred sailors. The men set sail from Spain, on course to Mexico, with boundless honor, glory, and riches before them.

Cortez landed his ships safely on the golden shores of the Yucatan, but his men were quickly overcome by fear as they gazed on the empire they were to attack. His small army realized that they were vastly outnumbered, and they were convinced that storming the glorified shores of the Aztec kingdom would surely result in their deaths. The frightened men pleaded with Cortez for a return to Spain and, when denied, plotted a mutinous takeover. They thought this conquest was impossible. Cortez came proudly before his men, ready to take them into battle, and offered them three simple, yet profound, words: "Burn the ships." He uttered it again: "Burn the ships." In order to ensure that his men were victorious, he urged them to burn away their option of failure. It was all or nothing. His men now had only one option: storm the shores, fight for victory, and in doing so, seize greatness.

Cortez told his men with certainty, "If we are going home, we are going home in their ships." The soldiers and sailors set their fleet aflame and stormed the seemingly unconquerable shores. There could be no looking back. The only way to any kind of life was now right in front of them: storm the shores or burn with the ships. They had no fallback position; they had no choice but to fight through what they thought was impossible.

For six centuries, no man had been successful in conquering the Aztecs, but Cortez's army, outnumbered and undertrained, did what no other army could do. They won. They overcame.

[Source: As shared with me by my father.]

This is the perfect picture of what it means to overcome. To me, overcoming means pressing on, no matter what, and never accepting failure as an option. It means never looking back. Once those men burned their ships, they didn't look back; they couldn't. Their focus was on what was in front of them—the task at hand. They no longer had a crutch to fall back on. They had no escape.

My diagnosis of PTS"d" was my crutch; it was my excuse for all my poor actions. I allowed that diagnosis to infect every part of my being and unknowingly began to allow it to not only control me but to define me. There was no significance in being diagnosed with PTSD—except for the significance that I gave it. My diagnosis was nothing more than a hurdle for me to overcome and to make a part of my past. It was a ship I had to burn.

Burning that ship was one the hardest things I have ever done. In order to burn it, I had to address it and come to the realization that I needed healing. Wounds that I never wanted to address needed to be reopened, cleaned out, and, once and for all, closed.

I made the decision to burn my ship in December 2014. I was sitting under an overpass on the highway with my Springfield 1911 .45 caliber pistol death-gripped in my lap. I had purchased my gun just months after returning to California in 2011. My wife and I had just moved into a nice little apartment in Carlsbad, and I needed the tools necessary to protect my wife, our house, and myself. The night I bought the gun, I slid it under my pillow and drifted off to sleep with it in my grips. I slept with gun in hand for months, but eventually I became okay with just keeping it under the pillow (much safer).

One night I awoke from a nightmare, standing naked in my living room, gun locked and loaded in the killing position, while my wife, in tears and afraid for her life, was calling out to me from the hallway. That night I made the decision to move the gun from under my pillow to under my mattress. The polished 1911 sat below my mattress for nearly a year before I engaged it again.

Aimee and I had gotten into an argument— I do not remember the reason for which we were fighting— but it ended with her getting in her truck and leaving. After I made a scene—and a fool of myself—in the parking lot of our apartment complex, she left, and I ran upstairs. I lifted the mattress and slid the gun into the bag I was packing. I grabbed the keys to my motorcycle and left home. I went up to the barracks on Camp Pendleton and spent the night staring at the beautiful pistol, wondering if pulling the trigger would magically solve everything. Aimee and I once again worked out the fight and "made up."

A few months later, we moved into a house on Camp Pendleton. I decided that I wouldn't keep my gun as readily available, so I locked it in a case and tucked it away below my bed. I never really took it out. For almost a year it just collected dust with the random other items that wound up stored under the bed. As the year went by, the gun moved yet again from under my bed to tucked in between a rack of sweaters on the top shelf of my closet. Also, as the year progressed, Aimee and I drifted further and further apart as I sunk deeper and deeper into my drug addiction and depression.

After we arrived at our marriage separation, I once again found myself staring at my gun, convincing myself that killing myself was my only option. I lived in my car for a few weeks and ended up couch crashing with some friends in San Diego. I made the deliberate choice not to kill myself—a choice that, at the time, I thought was huge, and that I was proud of myself for making. I even went as far as taking my gun to my friend's parents' house, where they locked it up. Another year went by, and I made some truly massive steps in the direction of healing. I kicked my drug habit; I started going to church; and I thought that I had "fixed" my problems. Actually (as I shared previously), I had just masked them and had buried them deep inside of me.

Aimee and I got back together, and my gun remained buried with my issues. Everything seemed to be going wonderfully: my marriage was back on track; we found out that we were having a son, and I started truly falling into a full-throttle career in my passion for music. My, how looks can be deceiving.

In December 2014, after I once again sabotaged my marriage and my life, I found myself covered in sweat under an overpass on the highway with my loaded .45 in hand.

I say all that to say this: no matter how far away from my gun I got and no matter how tightly I sealed it away, it was always there. Even though it was out of my house, I never got rid of it. My wounds were much like my gun: no matter how deeply I sealed them away or hid them beneath my masks, they were still present.

Unless my gun is gone, forever, it will always have not only the potential but also the opportunity to resurface and kill. I needed to not only address my need for healing but also destroy the things that were holding me back from true healing, once and for all.

It was 2012, and I was aimlessly walking around the halls of Wounded Warrior Battalion, awaiting my next appointment. I made my way over to the music room, where I was approached by a man and his wife. Chad and Kathy Robichaux are the ultimate tag team, helping warriors fight their demons and discover healing through finding and establishing a personal relationship with Christ. Chad was a Marine Corps combat veteran with Force Recon Battalion. After his multiple deployments, he too came home a changed man and subsequently found himself in a rapid downward spiral of chaos and self-sabotage. Through Christ, he found his way to overcoming his demons and finding true life. He began a foundation for wounded veterans called Mighty Oaks Warrior Programs, and he embarked on his calling into ministry.

He and his wife were at Camp Pendleton, giving away signed copies of his book, *Redeployed,* and enlisting warriors to come take part in his six-day healing program. He talked; I listened; he signed me up; I agreed. And he confirmed my attendance twice.

Then I blocked his number and tried acting like I had never met the guy.

In January 2015, I got another e-mail from the Mighty Oaks Foundation, asking me if I was still interested in attending their six-day program at a twenty-thousand-acre ranch on the Central Coast of California (this happened only weeks after I sat hopelessly in my truck, ready to once again attempt to end it all). There was no way that I could just chalk this up to coincidence, so I quickly responded with a yes, and by the end of the day, I was signed up and accepted into the program.

On January 18, I loaded my truck and drove from San Diego, five hours up the coast, to San Luis Obispo, CA, to the Sky Rose Ranch. I was scared to death pulling in. I had been to rehab, and I had been to both AA and NA programs, and the memories of my failed attempts at healing haunted me. In my head, I was worthless and I was a failure, especially when it came to healing. Nothing had worked for me in the past, and as I sat in my truck outside the ranch, my past failures swept over me, and I felt weak for thinking like that. I felt weak for asking for help. I felt weak because I couldn't do it on my own anymore. I felt weak for acknowledging my pain. I felt weak for admitting that I needed help. I felt weak for feeling weak.

I had never willingly signed up for something like this: six days of not only talking about my deepest feelings but talking about Jesus. Jesus was not a guy I wanted to talk about, primarily because Jesus was the easiest place for me to put the blame for...well, everything. "It's not my fault; it's God's fault."

I grew up in a Christian home. I was raised going to church. I was enrolled in a private Christian school from kindergarten to graduation, and after a year in public state college, I attended a Christian university. It was there that I fell victim to *religion*. Once I joined the Marines, I acquired a bad taste in my mouth for religion, and I embarked on my own journey, free from the constricting guidelines of spirituality. I still wore the mask though—on Sundays when I went to church—so that my Facebook friends and family wouldn't throw me into the "gone astray" category.

Because of my knowledge of the Bible and of Jesus, it was very easy for me to blame Him for everything that was going wrong around me. I questioned God more than ever during my deployment and in the years to follow. How could a just God allow this much evil in the world? How could a loving God allow war to unceasingly sweep over nations? If God truly loved me, why did He allow this to happen to me?

Rather than actually seeking the answers to my questions, I buried them beneath the weight of my newfound denial and hatred of a true and just God. I was 100 percent disinterested in obtaining a relationship with Christ, and I knew that this six-day program I was about to walk into was all about engaging healing head on via the pathway of finding and establishing a personal relationship with God.

I was a broken man—that was undeniable—and the thought of having even the slightest chance of hope again was enough to ignite a change for the better. I had tried for nearly five years to heal on my own and to hopelessly piece my shattered life back together. It was time to try something new. What was the worst thing that could happen?

On the first meeting of the first day, the program's manager took center stage and welcomed us to the ranch. I was surrounded by brothers, all of whom had been on combat tours, and all had come to the ranch for the same reason: brokenness in search of healing. To be honest with you, I have never felt stronger. There was no weakness in asking for help, and there was no shame in acknowledging my pains and troubles.

> *There was no weakness in asking for help, and there was no shame in acknowledging my pains and troubles.*

On the night of January 27, 2015, five days into my stay at Sky Rose Ranch, I surrendered my pain to Christ and wholly gave Him my broken life to be made complete and new.

Entering into a personal relationship with Jesus Christ did not cure me of post-traumatic stress;

believe me when I tell you that it is still an active occurrence in my daily life. But now, what I am able to do is to see through it for what it really is: a beautifully tragic part of my story. Am I healed? No, no I am not, but I *am* healing, and through Christ I am now overcoming.

"Live ~~like you're dying~~"

Three times I chose suicide, and three times I nearly threw away everything. I came to a point in my life at which I couldn't see past the pain, and I couldn't see anything but darkness.

In the year 2010, 630 warriors, including myself, were blown up by IEDs; in that same year, 499 of my brothers and sisters lost their heroic lives in Afghanistan, fighting for this beautiful country.

I look back on my best friend's death, and though it still pains me to even think about it, there is honor and pride in my heart for him. He lived an incredible life and died a hero's death. I am proud of Julio, and I am proud of all the warriors in my military family who sacrificed their lives in the name of freedom. What pains me the most, though, is the number of friends who have successfully stolen their own lives in suicide.

The last report I read told that twenty-two veterans a day were committing suicide. Five—and now that I'm revising this chapter I must unfortunately change that five to a six—six of my personal friends have chosen that route, and it's devastating. Too many people see death as the only valid option. I know; I've been there, and I have felt those very thoughts. And I'd be lying to you if I told you that those thoughts effortlessly go away. Though I am no longer a suicidal person, the thought and idea of suicide hauntingly creeps in at the most precise times. I once saw death as not only a beautiful escape but also as my *only* route to freedom.

I can honestly tell you that I once viewed suicide as the ultimate selfless act, mainly because I felt as though I was such a heavy burden to others. I was so convinced that if I were out of the equation, my family, my friends, and all those around me would be better off. I was a train wreck, and I couldn't allow those I loved to be destroyed with me in the wake of my impending crash.

There is so, *so* much beauty in this world, and there are so many good things that we would miss out on if we were to cut our lives short. I know it's much easier said than done, but all you have to do is live past the darkness and see it.

The key here, though, is *live*.

When I was in the thick of my hardships and in the darkest of my hours, it was nearly impossible to see any form of goodness coming in the future; but it did, and it still continues.

The way I see it, living with my diagnosis of PTSD never gets easier, but when I found something that gave me hope, it *did* get better. Don't get me wrong; it's still difficult. It's just a little better.

I found hope in life. Even though I found hope in living, I discovered that there is a fine line between being alive and living full of life. Just because we have a heartbeat doesn't mean that we are living; it just means that we exist. The life we live is filled, often to the brim, with struggles and pain, and unfortunately, we allow those things to take over and block out everything that is good and beautiful in life.

Our country went to war in Afghanistan, and what does the news broadcast on a daily account? They showcase nothing but the ugliness of war. We miss out on so much beauty when we focus on the bad.

Sometimes the darkness is far more blinding than the light. But sometimes, sometimes it takes a little darkness for us to be able to truly see and appreciate the beauty in the light.

One of the earliest memories I have of my childhood goes way back to my kindergarten days. Kindergarten was, and is, a year of discovery; at least, that's how I remember it. It was the year I discovered that girls actually didn't have cooties, and I inevitably got struck with my first crush. It was the year I discovered that "–ley"

> *Sometimes the darkness is far more blinding than the light. But sometimes, sometimes it takes a little darkness for us to be able to truly see and appreciate the beauty in the light.*

was actually apart of my first name and not my first middle name, and that the "–ley" that followed the "Brad" actually wasn't interchangeable and didn't work as "Brad Christian Fiteley." This was truly a life-changing discovery for a little boy in kindergarten!

It was also the year in which I saw my first solar eclipse. During craft time, my teacher had us assemble special glasses that we could wear outside so that we could look at the eclipse without harming our eyes. They were really awesome homemade sunglasses. I thought they were just the coolest and actually wore them quite often after that day! When our class went outside, we put our darkened lenses on and stared right up into the sun, looking directly at the most blinding light possible. Through darkness, we saw light.

Through darkness, I saw something beautiful.

In 2010, the road on which I was blown up was nothing but dangerous dust and rock-filled terrain. I bet you've seen the devastation of Afghanistan on the news, but I bet you didn't know that the road I was blown up on is now paved with painted lane lines and even has street lights erected on it. My bomb was the last bomb to ever kill on that road. Because of that horrific event on July 20, the local village came together and stood up against the Taliban. Now that road is fixed, and the people of Afghanistan have that much more safety secreted in their daily life. That's beautiful.

While I was deployed, there was no school for the children of Marjah. We worked tirelessly to create a safe environment for a school to be built. Well, the school was built, and children safely attend classes there now. Public, democratic elections were held in 2013—for the first time in the history of Marjah—and a leader was *chosen* by the people. They are no longer deemed property of the Taliban; rather, they can call themselves free people. That is true beauty, finally shining brightly after years and years of darkness.

"Live like your dyin'." Ever heard that little saying before? Sure you have. I have. You've probably even taken that phrase and lived it out loud, like I did. Not only is it the plot of numerous hit songs, but it's also a way of life that is adopted by many. I know I took it to heart, and that's how I "lived."

I had a fear, during the first years that I was back home, that somehow, in some way, at some point before tomorrow came, I would die. So I said, "Screw it." I excused my way of living by claiming that I was *truly living:* "seizing the moment!" I came close to dying, so I now choose to live, because I might not get a tomorrow. While living only for today may seem like a wildly fun thing to do, it's dangerous, and it's a slippery slope.

I don't want to live like I'm dying. I want to live today like I'm going to be alive tomorrow...and the next day...and the next day...and the next. That doesn't mean that I can't enjoy my moments and be present in the time I am in now, but it means that I have a legacy to live for. I have a life to live, and in no way, shape, or form will I ever cut that short. What if we all lived like we were going to live as opposed to living like we were going to die? I'm talking about really, truly living—knowing and intentionally anticipating that I will wake up to another day! Obviously, at some point we all will die, but I want to make it a point to live as much as I can before that day comes.

L ive and know. Choosing life: daily and actively making a choice to press on no matter what; to vow to never give up. That's a tough choice, but it's a choice that's worth the work. I promise you that.

It took me so long to start living my life again, and it took me acknowledging that I needed healing, and that I needed help. I am trained and ultimately programmed to consider myself nothing short of bulletproof—an invincible and unrelenting warrior, void of emotions and any form of weakness; trained to kill as easily and as instinctively as I breathe. I made the mistake of believing that seeking out help was admitting to weakness and that acknowledging my pain was essentially admitting that I was a failure. I continued to tell myself that I could do it on my own. I couldn't have been more wrong.

Seeking help took more strength than I knew I had. Talking to my wife about the things that I suppressed in my mind took more power and more work than I ever imagined; but the outcome was just as unimaginably amazing. Taking care of myself and seeking help does not mean that I am weak; it proves that I am a powerful being.

It took me quite a while to figure out what worked for me, but when I did, I stuck with it and saw it through. I was never good at sitting down with a therapist and talking through my issues. I became adept at just saying what I knew he or she wanted to hear; I pretty much just skated emotionlessly through all of my sessions. I was a trained liar, so I was good at making my therapists believe that they were actually helping me. I went through fourteen therapists until I found someone that I actually vibed with; and even still, weekly sessions with him aren't an easy thing to get through. For me, what really worked was music. For you, it may be something else, but you owe it to yourself to find out what works and to stop at nothing in order to find it.

> *Taking care of myself and seeking help does not mean that I am weak; it proves that I am a powerful being.*

There's a reason I have the words *Live & Know* forever tattooed on my body. They have come to mean more to me than I could have ever imagined. I will explain, but first, let me tell you a story that will help you understand this a little better.

There's this crazy, wild theory called the "Chaos Theory"; most people know it more commonly as the "Butterfly Effect." In 1961, a brilliant scientist by the name of Edward Lorenz was studying weather patterns, specifically those of hurricanes. He used a numerical system to plot his findings, and on one specific plotting, instead of typing in the entire number of the sequence, which was 0.506127, he rounded the number to 0.506 (a seemingly harmless thing to do); however, his results were vastly different because of it. Thus, he theorized the butterfly effect.

What he found was that the even the tiniest flap of a butterfly's wings in Brazil could be the deciding factor by which a tornado struck in the United States. Something as small and as meaningless as a butterfly flapping its wings could create just enough change in the atmosphere to completely change the course of a massive storm across the world. The action of the butterfly's wings was *not* directly what caused the storm, but it was a factor that contributed, early on, in the making of it.

[Source: Wikipedia.]

I look back on my life, as crazy and wild as it was. What if I did one tiny thing differently? What if...?

In 2007, I shattered my face in a cage fight, thus ending my very bright and hopeful career in the United States Air Force. Well, you know what happened next: I walked into the recruiting station. What if the Army would have been able to talk me into joining? What would have happened should I have chosen the Navy's office? Little things, little choices, seemingly thoughtless choices, led me to the Marine Corps office.

The day I left for boot camp at Parris Island, my recruiter called me twenty minutes prior to see if I could go early. What if I had chosen to be honest with him? What would have happened if I had told him that I had a 103-degree fever and was sick as a dog and probably should just wait until the next platoon started up in February? Well, I wouldn't have graduated in April, which put me through all my schooling after boot camp by July and led me to 3rd Amphibious Assault Battalion precisely at a time when they were looking for Marines to join a specific team preparing to deploy to Afghanistan.

If I hadn't shown up to my command at just the right time, I never would have been selected to train to go to war when I did. But wait a second here. Wouldn't that have been a good thing? Wouldn't that have meant that I wouldn't have gone to Afghanistan, ultimately placing me directly on a dirt road, driving toward a massive bomb hidden beneath it? Yeah, that's exactly what that means.

Let's keep going though. If I never would have gone on that specific deployment, I never would have been blown up, which sounds pretty rad, until I see where getting blown up has led me. It's because I got blown up that my body was broken, absolutely and completely. If I would not have been blown up and injured as specifically as I was, I would never have been transferred to the spinal specialists at the Richmond, Virginia, Spinal Polytrauma Unit, where I met Aimee. It was there that I started dating her, which led me to marrying her, which led us to having a son, which led me to where I am now: sitting here writing this book, as my beautiful baby boy sleeps in the next room.

Yes, getting blown up by a bomb sucked. It sucked a *lot*. I went through the most extreme pain that I have ever known, both physically and mentally, because of that bomb. Choices thereafter crashed me into drug addictions, suicide attempts, and the darkest depression imaginable. The deployment that made me question everything about life, about the world in which we live, and about my God forced me into a fate of mental warfare for what seemed like the rest of my life.

But still, if just one singular thing on my pathway through the darkness were to have been done differently—if I had reacted even the least bit differently to any one of those situations—I have no idea where I would be. But I do know that I wouldn't be where I am right now, and I wouldn't change where I am right now for anything. I get to look at my son, and I see life—beautiful, innocent, sweet, and alarmingly poopy at times but, overall, just an amazing life. I watched and experienced firsthand my son coming into our world: literally, life coming after the enormous wake of death. I have never felt such incredible emotions and love like this, and let me tell you, it's worth everything it took to get me here. Life is worth it, and regardless of what you personally believe, at the center of life, there's love, and unconditional love is an amazing thing that every single living person is deserving of.

> *It's worth everything it took to get me here.*

I will always have PTSD. I also know that I will always be mindlessly labeled as "sick." And you know what? I'm okay with it. PTSD does not define me. It used to, back when I made the choice to allow it to, but no longer is PTSD the excuse for my past, nor is it the chain holding me back from my bright and hopeful future. I choose to wear the fiery scars of my tragedies proudly. I choose to fearlessly *live* my life in honor of those that have gone before me. I live purposefully for all of those that are sure to follow. It is my choice to live and mine alone. I am writing you as living proof of the fact that there is indeed life after death.

Never quit.

Never surrender.

I choose life—every time. I hope and pray that you choose the same.

—Brad

A PERSONAL NOTE TO MY BROTHERS AND SISTERS

After I sought, chased, found, and captured healing—and I mean *true healing*—my life was radically changed. I am not the person I was before the war, nor do I ever expect to be, but I am something so much more now. I care. I love. I laugh. I smile. I feel—oh my goodness, how I feel. I *feel* everything: I feel joy. I feel happiness. I feel every experience in every passing day. I am what you may call a "social butterfly."

I also feel sadness: I still feel hurt. I still experience pain. I still doubt. I cry. I bleed. I still feel fear lurking around me. I still miss my brothers that gave the ultimate sacrifice. The difference now is that those "bad" feelings do not overpower me; rather, they *empower* me. They empower me to seize life in every facet of living. They make me stronger. The feelings that *are* life are meant to be felt, not numbed.

Without sadness there would be no beauty in happiness. Without pain there would be no such thing as strength. And you, my brothers and sisters, are mighty because of the pain and struggle that have made you that way.

> Without sadness there would be no beauty in happiness. Without pain there would be no such thing as strength.

I did not want to lose the crutch of my PTSD diagnosis, because in doing that, it meant that I had to assume the personal responsibility for all of my actions. I had to remove the opportunity of having something besides myself to blame. I chose drug addiction. I chose self-sabotage. I chose divorce. I chose hate. I chose unforgiveness. I chose death. And in doing so, I chose defeat.

It's easy to be sick; getting well is the hard part. One of my dear brothers is currently diagnosed with stage four non-Hodgkin's lymphoma, a rare and deadly cancer. He did not choose that sickness to infiltrate his body, but he *did* choose to unremittingly fight the cancer and to never give up, despite the slim chances of survival.

When it comes to sickness, you generally have two options: succumb to it or fight it and heal. I did not choose a lifelong diagnosis of PTSD, but it happened. I was labeled as sick, and I chose to succumb to that sickness. For so long I was told to just learn to live with PTSD. I was told that I would never heal, so why try. I was told that PTSD was a timeless beast that would haunt me to the death.

Once I was told that I had a choice and that I *could* indeed fight this monster, I entered the fight.

You have a choice, right now, in this moment. You *can* indeed fight this monster. You have a choice to fight for your life, so fight for it. Look to your left and right and look at the family we have. We are brothers. We are sisters. Together we can stand tall and make an extraordinary difference in this world.

We are molded to be leaders, not isolated in depression. We were trained to be fighters, so let's fight. We fought, and many died, in order for this beautiful nation to remain free, so let us not revoke and diminish our own freedom to this enemy labeled PTSD. We earned the title *veteran*, so let us not claim the title *victim*.

Some things are worth fighting for, and you—you are worth the fight. I will fight. Will you?

—Your brother, Brad

KEY THOUGHTS TO REMEMBER

Use these pages to write down key thoughts or ideas that you
want to remember from the book.

BRAD C. FITE

ABOUT THE AUTHOR

When Brad Fite left his collegiate life in Michigan (where he was pursuing a degree in Music Business) to enlist in the United States Marine Corps, his story became anything but predictable.

In July 2010, while conducting a combat patrol in Afghanistan, a roadside bomb detonated directly beneath him, causing catastrophic injuries that warranted him the Purple Heart. His physical array of injuries would heal, but the invisible wounds would haunt him for years. While recovering in multiple hospitals, Brad's misfortunate fame began to take its toll in the form of PTSD.

After three failed suicide attempts, Brad delved back into music and discovered that through music he could begin healing.

After attending an Entrepreneurship Bootcamp for Veterans with Disabilities at Syracuse University,

Brad graduated with honors and began operating Warriors Song, his foundation for music therapy.

Now a successful entrepreneur, motivational speaker, author of the book *Life after Death: A Survivor's Story*, music recording artist, global humanitarian, and contributor of service to such organizations as the USO, Phoenix Patriot Foundation, Global Sound Lodge, and Hope for the Arts, Brad is sought after by nonprofits and businesses alike to take their audiences to the next level. Brad's willingness to share the vulnerability brought on by his life-changing injuries in war through his story and through music brings a broad appeal. His can-do attitude and hope-filled journey inspire and engage those he leads, and this carries into his motivational speaking for numerous organizations.

Brad Fite is widely acknowledged as an advocate for those who can no longer fight for themselves. And they know, as all who meet him do, that Brad Fite fights the battle until he wins.

If you or someone you know is struggling
with post-combat trauma,
Mighty Oaks Warrior Programs
is a great resource.

You can learn more and also apply for their program
at https://www.MightyOaksPrograms.org.

To contact Brad C. Fite:

LifeafterDeathBook@gmail.com

To follow the Facebook page:

https://www.facebook.com/LifeafterDeathBook

To contact Brad's editor for permission to use
extended quotations from the book or for information
regarding how to purchase books in quantity:

Brenda@PEPWritingServices.com